PRAISE FOR
UNPACKING BLISS

I0153186

"*Unpacking Bliss: The Suitcase Theory of Life* is an extraordinary guide to discovering the flow you were born to live in. Sandi and Stacie don't just offer wisdom; they offer a transformation. They invite you to step beyond the patterns that have kept you stuck and into a life where your natural genius leads the way. With the perfect blend of practical tools and deep spiritual insight, this book gives you the clarity, confidence, and connection to align with your highest path. If you're ready to move from striving to thriving, this is your map to a life of purpose, fulfillment, and joy.

– **Roger James Hamilton**, Founder, Genius Group, NY Times Best Selling Author, Creator of Wealth Dynamics and Talent Dynamics

"*Unpacking Bliss* is a loving invitation to (re)connect with your voice, discover your superpowers, and speak your truth even when, and especially when, life is messy. It's a treasure trove of wisdom on how to release the need for control and certainty, cultivate deeper self-compassion and self-trust, and take radical ownership of your life. It's a must-read!"

– **Alexia Vernon**, executive communication coach and author of *Step into Your Moxie: Amplify Your Voice, Visibility, and Influence in the World*

"The beating heart of *Unpacking Bliss* is the belief that all of us can find joy and bliss. Thank you Sandi and Stacie for sharing with us how to pack our suitcases with purpose, self-trust and core values. Your book lifted my spirit!

– **Dr. Arthur Schwartz**, President, Character.org

"*Unpacking Bliss* is an inspiring roadmap for anyone seeking to navigate life's twists and turns with resilience and joy. With heartfelt stories and actionable guideposts, this book empowers readers to unpack emotional baggage, rediscover their innate bliss, and build a life of fulfillment. I've had the privilege of working with Sandi and Stacie, witnessing them birth their businesses and visions. They are exceptional leaders creating a wave of impact that is long overdue. Their stories not only inspire but also compel you to join their movement. This book is a must-read for anyone ready to transform their life and embrace their innate bliss.

– **Lisa Chastain**, thought leader, best-selling author, personal finance expert, host of The Real Money Podcast, and keynote speaker helping women transform their relationship with money and achieve financial success.

"Tender and strong. Inner and outer. Story and teaching. *Unpacking Bliss* is metaphorical salve for a hurting world ready for change. A beautiful read I highly recommend!"

– **Dr. Darcy Lord**, Self-Love Expert & Owner Programs That Uplift

"*Unpacking Bliss: The Suitcase Theory of Life* is a powerful declaration of Sandi and Stacie's 'Why Not Now?' moment. As co-authors, they courageously share their journeys, unpacking the lessons, tools, and truths that empower us to live with intention and authenticity. Drawing from experiences like our time together in the Renegade Collective and inspired by Tony Hsieh's legacy of creativity and connectedness, this book invites readers to step boldly into their own 'Why Not Now?' moments. It's a guide to finding joy, meaning, and purpose in every chapter of life."

– **Amy Jo Martin**, Founder/CEO of Renegade Global, NY Times Bestselling Author & host of Why Not Now? Podcast

"*Unpacking Bliss* is like having a deep, unfiltered conversation with a friend who's been through it all and wants to see you thrive. The Herrera Sisters lay it all out— honest, raw, and refreshingly real. Their stories and tools make you stop and think, 'OK, I can definitely do this!' If you're feeling stuck, carrying emotional baggage, or just need a reminder of your own power, this book delivers the clarity and courage to move forward.

– **Danielle Ford**, member of the Nevada State Board of Education and advocate for innovative, student-centered educational change

UNPACKING BLISS

Unpacking
BLISS
The Suitcase Theory of Life

The Herrera Sisters
Dr. Stacie Herrera & Sandi Herrera

Unpacking Bliss: The Suitcase Theory of Life
© 2025 by Stacie Hererra and Sandi Hererra

Library of Congress Control Number: 2024921608

ISBN: 978-1-964686-21-9 (paperback)   978-1-964686-22-6 (ebook)

Although this publication is designed to provide accurate information about the subject matter, the publisher and the author assume no responsibility for any errors, inaccuracies, omissions, or inconsistencies herein. This publication is intended as a resource, however, it is not intended as a replacement for direct and personalized professional services.

Editors: Mary Ward Menke, Dianna Graveman
Cover and Interior Design: Emma Elzinga

Printed in the United States of America

First Edition

3 West Garden Street, Ste. 718
Pensacola, FL 32502
www.indigoriverpublishing.com

Ordering Information:

Quantity sales: Special discounts are available on quantity purchases by corporations, associations, and others. For details, contact the publisher at the address above.

Orders by US trade bookstores and wholesalers: Please contact the publisher at the address above.

With Indigo River Publishing, you can always expect great books, strong voices, and meaningful messages. Most importantly, you'll always find . . . *words worth reading.*

CONTENTS

"The privilege of a lifetime is to become who you really are."
– Carl Jung

INTRODUCTION

We are so grateful that you are here, as the Herrera Sisters we want to thank you for joining us along this journey. We've spent over twenty years cultivating these experiences and learning and growing together. We wrote this book for you, as these are lessons we wish we would've learned sooner. Along the way, we found so much growth and learning for ourselves and within our relationship as sisters. We hope this inspires your growth and learning as we all journey this path together.

Dr. Stacie Herrera and Sandi Herrera

www.humanizedu.com
www.herrerasisters.com

THE ROADMAP

It was early spring in 1984. We were heading down the mountain to visit Nana and Grandpa, as we did most weekends. It felt like any other trip—until all of a sudden Mom swerved to avoid the barrage of falling rocks heading straight toward us. The sound of rocks hitting the road echoed all around us; then we felt another jolt as a boulder struck the side of our car.

Mom slammed on the brakes, weaved to avoid an oncoming car, and then punched the accelerator to rocket past the stream of dirt sliding toward us at an unfathomable speed. We bounced around in the back of the Subaru station wagon, feeling as if we were in a pinball machine, holding on for dear life. There was an awful sound coming from beneath the car as it dragged something along with us as we raced to safety.

And then suddenly, we stopped. A line of cars extended down the road in the other lane, traffic halted by the landslide.

The look on the faces of the oncoming drivers was of disbelief, as if they were thinking, "How did you make it through that?"

Of course we made it through. Mom knew there was only one way to get out of that situation alive, and that was to bravely listen to her intuition and drive like hell to keep her children safe.

We made it out of the landslide mostly intact. The dragging noise had come from a boulder wedged into the chassis. Dislodging the debris, we took stock of the situation. There was only one thing to do:

keep going. Scrambling back into the car, Mom put the car in drive, and we continued to our grandparents' house.

⚬§

Nana and Grandpa's had always been an oasis of safety, care, and predictability. We loved that. Nana cooked for us and taught us how to be creative, always setting us up with arts, crafts, and other fun learning activities. When Grandpa left for work in the wee hours of the morning, he'd wake us so we could crawl into his spot in the bed next to Nana. The weekend of the landslide was no different, but after the insanity we'd endured, it felt like we'd exited a vortex and landed in a safe haven. We were cared for. We were safe.

⚬§

Growing up in Big Bear, California, high in the San Bernardino Mountains, we spent our childhood in motion, navigating through various vortices from chaos to traumatic situations to calm peaceful predictability. We lived mostly with our mom and spent a lot of weekends with our maternal grandparents at their house in Norwalk, California—a two-hour drive down the mountain. The weekends we didn't spend with our grandparents were spent with our dad. He was often studying for his private pilot's license, or to be promoted within the fire department, or to improve his construction skills. When Dad was working or studying, we stayed with Grandma Lupe, our paternal grandmother, who provided another safe haven among our cousins. We weren't always able to communicate with her well because she only spoke Spanish, and we often depended on our cousins to clue us in.

⚬§

Our parents divorced when Sandi was eighteen months old. From that time forward—and especially when Mom was married to our stepdad—our childhoods were riddled with uncertainty and fear. We rarely felt grounded or knew what lay ahead.

The most intense years began when we were three and five years old and lasted until we were nine and eleven—the most impactful imprinting years in child development. We often found ourselves running fearfully up the stairs of our little A-frame house to hide from the noisy assault of yelling, fighting, slamming doors, and smashing objects. The aggression usually ended with our stepdad screeching out of the driveway, his tires kicking up a stream of driveway rocks as he sped away. The sound of Mom crying told us the coast was clear. We could now make sure she was okay and help clean up the aftermath of yet another explosive event.

As if our preschool and elementary years weren't chaotic enough, middle and high school came with the constant instability of being raised by a single mother. During the week, like many other Gen Xers, we were latchkey kids left to our own devices, often taking care of ourselves while our mom was at work. Mom tried her best to make ends meet, but that meant moving us around through eight different houses in the sixteen years we lived in Big Bear and frequently standing in line for government support. Through all of that, Mom battled her own traumas, creating an incredibly shaky foundation for all of us.

Our youngest sister, Stephanie, was born into this environment in 1982 as the only child of our mother and stepdad. Enduring everything as sisters thrown into these situations united us in knowing we had each other, even when there were sibling bumps in the road.

In a whirlwind of shifting circumstances, we spent a lot of time riding up and down the curvy mountain roads. To make these wild and nauseating trips more manageable, we made them fun. We'd lay down the seats in the back of the old Subaru station wagon, unroll our sleeping bags, and climb inside them. As the car wound through hairpin turns, we'd slide back and forth over the nylon fabric, swishing as our sleeping bags slid over the upholstery. We surfed the turns on the road just as we rode the waves of our family life, doing our best to enjoy the ride and not get carsick. Sometimes we hit major obstacles.

In time, we learned how to adapt and find our unique ways to thrive.

Life is a bit like that. We encounter all sorts of unexpected situations. Sometimes the best choice is to stop and reassess the situation. Occasionally, we have to find an alternate route. Once in a while, an obstacle halts our progress. And other times, when we find ourselves staring at the possibility of being swept off a cliff, we put the pedal to the floor to save our life, even if that means doing something terrifying in the process.

As we navigate these twists and turns, we occasionally pick up heavy baggage—sort of like the boulder we'd snagged in our escape from the landslide. Most of the time, though, we collect extra odds and ends a little at a time, tucking things into our suitcases, not recognizing the burden of that accumulation until we're exhausted from carrying it.

GUIDING YOUR JOURNEY THROUGH THESE PAGES

When we boil down the resistance and hesitation to divulge all of the experiences and the impact of the challenging and traumatic periods of our lives, the sticking point is trust: trusting you, the reader, with our stories, knowing that you may judge our experience based upon the limited information presented within this book. You may wonder why we have glossed over some experiences and highlighted others in greater detail. This book is not meant to be a memoir, yet we understand that reflection and integrating learning requires seeing yourself or in some way relating to the story. Our vulnerability in sharing examples from our lives is to assist in developing your trust in the wisdom we are sharing as you navigate through these pages along your unique journey.

On our journey, we have invested in multiple healing modalities to be able to shift our stories from "There is something wrong with me" through "Something happened to me" to "This is what's right with me."

This book is best used after healing from any significant trauma in your life. If reading this book causes significant unease or discomfort, it may be a signal that you need to invest in further healing. We know that healing looks different for everyone. Please reach out to a therapist, spiritual leader, or trusted advisor for guidance.

Ultimately, this book is a companion to living a more fulfilled, healthier life while finding a sustainable path back to your blissful, true self. We hope to help you lighten your load and show you some ways to help navigate the path with ease and grace. You may decide to take notes or visit some sections multiple times. *Unpacking Bliss* doesn't always follow the linear fashion we've outlined here. Key Nuggets of wisdom appear at the end of each chapter to assist in navigating your way. Your journey is unique to you, and we hope our journey can help you take away nuggets that inspire you and act as a compass to the bliss you desire in the time that is most aligned to your path.

FINDING BLISS

Where is bliss? Some people associate bliss with the feeling of joy and contentment. Some spend their entire lives seeking bliss. Although bliss is not a destination, we crave finding it. We buy countless books, attend classes and spiritual sessions, and integrate habits and rituals into our daily lives to find it, to feel it. After our collective struggles of the last few years, we all deserve bountiful moments of bliss. Many ancient teachings remind us that we ARE bliss. In life, we're challenged by twists and turns, and those, at times, cloud our thinking and our ability to experience blissful moments. When we have clarity, we know this to be true: bliss is innate.

We wrote this book to share the wisdom that we've gathered along our journey to help us all remember the bliss that resides within.

Bliss is deep within us; it is the journey of our lives to rediscover it. Please join us on our journey as we share stories of our discovery.

WHO "WE" ARE

From Stacie: Meet My Little Sister, Sandi

As a ten-year-old, I would have described my younger sister with words like stubborn, strong-willed, someone who always gets her way. As an adult, I can see those early traits have morphed in a beautifully positive way: she is a trailblazer, relentlessly compassionate, strong, and a visionary leader. In my eyes, Sandi's superpower is connecting humans to big ideas. She has charisma; you can feel it as soon as she walks into the room. Sandi can read the energy of a group of people and uplift them, excite them, or ground them, all in an effort to ignite self-awareness and collective growth.

I love traveling to new places with her by my side. As children, we traveled by cars, trains, and planes to family reunions in Kansas and on trips with Dad to Colorado and Mexico, navigating her motion sickness along the way.

One of my most cherished memories is when Sandi flew to Moscow, Russia, to spend two weeks with me during my junior year abroad in college. Having my sister join me during a time that felt so life-changing was a beautiful gift. Sandi trusted me to translate for her and guide her through a completely unfamiliar country. That faith strengthened our bond and highlighted her adventurous spirit. It was the start of a lifetime of travel adventures to faraway places. (For the record, Sandi has been to more countries than I have . . . for now).

Although Sandi is quite comfortable waiting until the last minute for travel logistics (transportation, housing—all the things I spend hours researching and strategizing about), she likes to have her living space in order and clean (something that is not always at the top of my priority list). We differ in slight ways yet align in our values and vision. This alignment allows us to provide each other with a safe place to be ourselves and to grow without limitations, something that flourishes because of our sisterhood. Sandi has been a witness to my entire life—something that only siblings share.

We share a thirst for knowledge that has led us to collecting information to live our best lives in structured and unstructured learning environments. Sandi graduated with a degree in business partially by default; she has always wanted to help others and dreamed of being a doctor, yet the rigidity of a premed track didn't exactly fit her need to innovate and create. Her business degree led her to a series of successful sales and leadership positions as a technical recruiter and a real estate broker before landing a unique opportunity to jump on the Delivering Happiness bus—assisting Zappos.com and Delivering Happiness founder and CEO Tony Hsieh and his team with corporate culture transformation. Sandi then spent two years becoming a certified Organization and Relationship Systems Coach, which deepened her commitment to supporting individuals, communities, and organizations.

This work led her to recognize the need for culture work within schools, making schools better places to work. Sandi found her niche helping the helpers: educators who are entrusted with our most precious gift, our children. As a mother who values education within a nurturing environment, Sandi recognized the importance of supporting teachers to ensure her son had the best learning environment possible. Sandi expanded her work to a number of schools in Las Vegas, Nevada, before introducing her work in Florida and California and then coaching educators globally.

I trust her with my children without question. She has created a bond as Aunt Sandi, a.k.a. Tía, that I cherish and admire. My children view her as one of the coolest people on the planet. They marvel at her adventurous spirit and authentic conversations. Sandi is so well-loved and admired that she is designated the primary trustee for guardianship on multiple family members' wills and trusts. She lives with a strong sense of family, nurtures relationships, and travels extensively to be present for all of us lucky enough to be related to her.

Sandi is my rock; more specifically, she is my geode—strong on the outside with a beautiful core of crystals that exude peace, kindness, and compassion. She is a literal mountain of ideas, one of which led to writing this book.

From Sandi: Meet My Big Sister, Stacie

The first time I heard the song "Wind Beneath My Wings," I was about ten years old and immediately knew that it was describing my sister. It felt weird to have such a visceral reaction to a song at such a young age, but I just knew it was about Stacie. I definitely hit the sister lottery when I was born as Stacie's little sister. From my earliest memory, she has been by my side with a steady strength, no matter what this crazy life has thrown our way.

Others describe her as having the power of a quiet storm and being a blanket of good. I also know the other side of her, the one that rolled her eyes each time I got to ride in the front seat of the car as we drove on the mountain roads of our hometown so I wouldn't throw up. Despite her sisterly irritation with me, if we were in a similar situation without our family, she would immediately advocate for me to sit in the front.

In high school, she was the first one to tell people all the ways I was succeeding when they referred to me as "Stacie's little sister." Meanwhile, she was the one kicking ass in all her classes, leading the pep rallies as our high school mascot, and participating in all the clubs and activities to ensure she would get into the college of her choice . . . rockstar!

Watching her raise her children with such love and generosity is beautiful. I will never forget the time we went to visit her family in Florida for the first time. We walked in, and Stacie immediately had these well-planned, engaging learning activities to ensure my son Hunter, who was two years old at the time, felt welcome. It gave us some much needed sister time while we watched our children play and learn.

Stacie achieved her doctorate in school psychology while simultaneously raising four gifted children who are not more than eighteen months apart in age. I learn so much every day witnessing her passion for mental health advocacy and her ability to illuminate the innate gifts in all children, guiding and inspiring them to own their inner brilliance. It's as if the wisdom of generations flows through her. She took a huge leap of faith to open her own practice, Herrera Psychology, providing individual therapy to children, which then propelled her to create a separate company that provided telehealth and psychology services in schools. She is dedicated to making sure no child goes unnoticed or undiagnosed and that every little one receives the resources they need to become thriving humans. I am incredibly grateful our career paths have merged and led us to cocreate comprehensive, sustainable, psychologically safe environments through our company, HumanizEDU, in which students and educators can work and learn. I can't imagine a better copilot on this path to making a difference in mental wellbeing around the globe, a shared passion we have discovered over the past decade.

I admire the deep wisdom my sister brings to everything she does. When she walks into a room, she exudes a warm kindness that allows others to immediately trust her. This intuitive superpower has led to the growth of her practice within the community while also attracting an incredible team. Together, they are driving the mission of innovating mental health from the inside out.

As a mother of four, business owner of two, and wife of one, her daily world is incredibly full of humans, logistics, and details that she passionately cares for. And when it all gets to be too much, she practices what she teaches by asking for support . . . and is known to be met at her car door on occasion with a glass of wine by her wonderful husband, who knows just what she needs at the end of a long day.

The Magic Between Us

In her work as a psychologist, Stacie has noticed an interesting pattern in the siblings she works with. When young siblings are faced with adversity, they tend to bond together, taking care of one another, almost as if it is them against the world. Siblings whose lives haven't been thrust into significant challenges often have more conflict between them. While this isn't always the case (there are lots of factors that impact sibling bonds), this was certainly true of our relationship.

As sisters, we have been linked by an impenetrable bond since we were born. Stacie remembers the moment when she realized she wasn't an only child anymore. It was Christmas morning, and she was two and a half. She received a child-sized play kitchen set, complete with a penguin refrigerator and a hippopotamus stove. Much to her disappointment, she was told that she had to share her gift with this other little being. Her dismay didn't last long, though. As we grew, so did our bond. It became one in which we both intuitively knew that protecting each other was our path to survival . . . even if sharing wasn't always easy for the first eighteen years.

Our experience growing up was not sunshine and rainbows; it was more of a moonlit night with beams of light and scary dark corners. While it was littered with adverse childhood experiences, our deep connection to each other and our playful exploration of the world helped cushion our childhood's sharp edges. Though we've always been close and knew we would be there for each other, we haven't always known how to communicate with each other from a heart-centered place. We would often avoid hard conversations and gloss over things in an attempt to not burden each other. Through the writing of this book and discovering our shared passions, we are on a healing journey to connect and communicate from an authentic, vulnerable place. It's definitely not always easy and so worth it to use our relationship as an anchor point of our bliss.

We have distinct memories of sitting at the top of the stairs with our arms around each other, waiting for the chaos of our mom and stepdad fighting downstairs to end. Finding safety and assessing situations for safety became part of our existence. Quietly listening to adult conversations and carefully watching body language and tone gave us valuable clues to navigate our home life. We didn't always know what was happening or how to deal with what was going on around us, but we knew we could depend on each other.

Sometimes we were told to go outside and play when things were getting heated. In fact, some of our most treasured childhood memories are of walking up to the end of the block where the national forest land butted up to our neighborhood. We'd nestle among the trees and rock formations and play. We imagined one particular rock formation was our house, complete with an imaginary kitchen, living room, a couple of bedrooms, and a deck that overlooked the forest. Not only were we safe, but we were having fun. Just as our mom was doing the best with what she had in an era when single moms (and moms in general) weren't well-supported, we made it our business to find joy and fun wherever we could.

We grew into adults and embarked upon our own separate journeys through careers, marriages, and raising children. One thing never changed: we found refuge in each other.

Perhaps because of the adversity we faced, we both pursued paths of developing our own self-awareness and a desire to help others find their way too. We have had amazing opportunities to learn ways to return to our own innate blissful state and to witness that in one another. We think this unique lens on growth and self-development will help make the space for you to explore your own journey.

We continue to bear witness to each other's innate strength and care. Sandi feels the need to be strong and not burden Stacie with having to take care of her. Meanwhile, Stacie wants to care for and protect Sandi but also sees her as incredibly strong. Our youngest sister, Stephanie, is often on the receiving end of extra mothering from both of us, as we continue to attempt to protect her from the chaos she was born into. We have been lucky to see all the concepts we've been learning and practicing over the years show up in each other.

THE TRAVELER'S JOURNEY

Like the road down the mountain where we grew up, the path of life is often a winding one. Sometimes, in fact, you'll have to backtrack or dash ahead. What's more, there is no endpoint. There is no "reaching enlightenment" and then kicking back with a margarita. Life is cyclical, and so is this journey we are all on to uncover our innate bliss. We trust that this concept of a cyclical journey inspires you and gives you permission to enjoy the ride. As you navigate the journey, we hope this book will help you find more ways to be playful and fulfilled in the process. We suspect that by the end, you will have let go of the focus on the destination because you'll be so smitten with the route.

We all have baggage. We can navigate the road blindly, carrying all the baggage we've picked up along the way, or we can work to remove the blinders, unpack the suitcase, and build a toolkit to help us navigate. Just like a seasoned business traveler who can navigate airports and train stations with a light carry-on and an easy manner, you too can begin to navigate the path differently.

The miraculous thing about this trip is that it is simultaneously inward and outward. The further we dive into ourselves to reach the innate joy at our core, the more we continue to grow outwardly.

Three Guideposts

There are three concepts that are foundational to the Traveler's Journey:

1. **Noticing:** Building the skill of observing ourselves, our behaviors, and our surroundings.

2. **Curious inquiry:** Thoughtfully and neutrally questioning what we've observed.

3. **Taking aligned action:** Using the data we've collected to make informed choices about the next step.

These steps will be nuanced in some of the chapters, but by the time you reach the end of this book, they will begin to feel natural. You'll likely begin to use them without thinking. You will be able to use these three guideposts as a strong foundation, enabling you to build a powerful life evolving through growth and bliss.

THE TOOLS

We are going to walk the path to unpacking bliss together. The following chapters lay out what we trust is an intuitive path. We've seen travelers navigate through these challenges and triumphs in roughly this direction. You, however, may find that your path looks a little different. Feel free to skip around or concentrate on the areas that resonate the most. You may find yourself skipping ahead or returning to previous chapters as you go—that's perfect. We hope this travelog will be a companion for you on all points of your journey.

Here's what you can expect: The first portion of the book focuses on looking inward and making adjustments to our vehicle in order to safely make our way. In Chapter 1, we begin at the beginning and explore the narratives we've told ourselves through unconscious patterning and limiting beliefs. From there, we can begin to understand our lens on the world in Chapter 2 through the study of the brain and how we've evolved as humans. Chapter 3 introduces the idea of thinking on purpose and using current knowledge in neuroscience to fuel our journey to bliss. When we've navigated thinking on purpose, we can begin to understand the ways in which we can give ourselves permission to be who we are in any given moment. We'll do that in Chapter 4.

The second section of the book is a subtle shift to looking outward. Now that we have learned about our inner mechanisms, we can begin to hone and shape them. Chapter 5 looks at the way in which we develop self-trust, which allows us to more confidently move in the world. This self-assuredness paves the way to uncovering and using our core values, which we'll learn about in Chapter 6. Our core values and self-trust are the fuel for our superpower, a concept we'll investigate in Chapter 7.

Once we've traversed these inner territories and seen how we can more joyously and authentically be in the world, we'll begin to explore the ways in which we shine that light. In Chapter 8, we'll look at our hardwired need for connection and belonging and how this journey can help us connect in meaningful ways. Finally, in Chapter 9, we'll summit the mountain and learn how to own our own bliss.

Each chapter will end with a list of the Key Nuggets you can gather and tuck away into your daypack. This will give you the highlights of the chapter for your reference.

While we are never in the same place twice, we often circle around to the same patterns again and again. Each time you revisit a challenge, you have an opportunity to employ what you've learned and practiced.

As we embarked upon the writing of this book, we faced some of our own patterns and stories, soft places and trigger points. We wrestled with being authentic, vulnerable, and open, and with considering our families' wellbeing. We reopened some old wounds and healed them further. We have gotten better at using the practices we're going to highlight for you in the following pages, but we aren't done. Part of this journey is recognizing that there is no such thing as "broken" or "fixed." We're all just works in progress, evolving as we grow.

Know that we are with you in spirit, as are thousands of others out there. You aren't alone on this path, and there is no wrong way to do it. We hope you'll trust us, but more importantly, trust yourself. The road to bliss may not always be well-paved, but with practice, we can find the way.

Big hugs!

Chapter 1

THE STORIES
WE TELL

SANDI: UNPACKING A CHILDHOOD STORY

Several years ago, I took a public speaking class. At the end of the first session, our instructor gave us a homework assignment: *Share the first time you remember having a voice.* We were to return the following week and share in front of the class.

I went home and began mulling it over. My mind ran in circles, ruminating over the question. I searched my memory bank but couldn't locate a suitable story. The truth is, I was stuck.

As the second session quickly approached and I hadn't completed the assignment, I started to panic. There I was, a professional woman who prided herself on being responsible and prepared, and I had absolutely nothing ready for class. As I drove there, heat and vibration seeped into my body, like every nerve was on fire. The sensation was nearly overwhelming. I wanted to ease that discomfort as soon as I could. I thought to myself: *I'll wing it. I just need to go first and get this over with.*

I found myself on the small platform at the front of the room, surrounded by a semicircle of thirteen other women. Heat continued to flush through me, and my face turned beet red. My voice shook as I introduced myself, and tears stung the edge of my throat. I couldn't re-member the first time I had a voice, but I did have a deep, crystal clear memory of being a silent three-year-old.

I crouched down on the stage, and suddenly I was that three-year-old again. I began to speak, and as I did, the memory flooded through me as though it were happening all over again.

"I stand outside my mother and stepfather's bedroom window next to the water spigot. They are filling their waterbed with the garden hose, and I am responsible for turning the water on and off when they ask. I desperately need to go to the bathroom."

I squeeze my eyes closed, remembering the pain and sharing, "I can't ask for a break to go to the bathroom because I'll get in trouble."

"Something warm and wet creeps down my legs, and shame burns my cheeks," I continued. "When the waterbed is full, I slip into the bathroom to clean up, determined to hide my shameful accident."

"I never tell anyone about it, but this experience plants the seed of belief that my needs are insignificant."

As I returned to the present moment with tears on my face, sur-rounded by supportive women, I recognized that this was a core wound. This wound has kept me from speaking up over and over in my lifetime. My disconnection with my own voice became a pattern.

I thought back to the experience of giving the graduation speech as senior class president. What a great honor, right? I had no recollection of that experience; I blacked it out entirely. I know I gave the speech, because I was a kid who did what was expected of her. But I have no memory of graduation. I disassociated completely with situations in which I had to use my voice.

I remember sitting at a boardroom table with twenty other people. I was the broker for a real estate development firm, and we were strat-egizing plans for an $800 million mixed-use project. I had all kinds of thoughts and ideas swirling in my head, but I just sat there and didn't contribute at all. The very thought of interjecting my voice into the conversation made my heart race and my face flush.

A few years later, I was asked to speak at a big Downtown Las Vegas Project community meeting on behalf of Delivering Happiness. I can't for the life of me remember what I said, only that when I got back to my seat, the person next to me said, "You're so red! Why do you get like that?"

I was so ashamed that the visceral sensation of being seen in public (turning red) distracted others from what I was actually saying, as if I had control over it.

While I've recognized my limiting belief, to this day I battle my nervous system to not fire and turn my whole body red when I even think of something that someone might judge me for. I have to remind myself over and over: *I am safe, I am safe, I am safe.* I wish I could just sweat or have a racing heart or something not so visible, but this is part of how I'm built.

When I shared this story with Stacie for the first time before we sat down to write this book, she watched me very closely.

"In elementary school, I would have an accident in the classroom once a year," she confessed. "I just assumed it wasn't okay to interrupt class to ask to go to the bathroom. It was ingrained in me that you do as you're told and don't advocate for your own needs."

THE IMPACT OF CHILDHOOD EXPERIENCES

Our childhood experiences give us data as little humans. Perhaps it's stories we gather from our role models. Sometimes we learn limiting beliefs based upon what we *don't* see. For example, if we never see someone who looks like us climbing a mountain, or running a science lab, we might think we can't do that either.

We collect this data into a suitcase, and it informs how we interact with the world. Throughout our lives, we keep that suitcase tucked under the bed and sometimes even forget that it's there, especially the hidden compartments we can struggle to open. When life gets rough, we pull it out to sort through. We unpack what's been stored away to determine what is essential and what isn't working anymore. This process lightens our load so we can more nimbly move along our journey to bliss. We do this throughout our lives, and in doing so, we grow.

There in that public speaking class, with her heart in her throat, Sandi was compelled to unpack this story. She was a little girl who could not speak up for her most basic needs. Not having a voice as a child led to years of not speaking up. If she did open her mouth to speak, she was flooded with uncomfortable sensations or disassociation from her body.

She knew she had work to do.

This experience prompted Sandi to examine the story and see how it wasn't serving her anymore. Like all of us, Sandi is a work in progress and has worked over the past two decades to reach a place where she can catch triggers as they occur and love herself for who she is.

Sandi's story about feeling she had no voice is just one example of how our beliefs are formed. We both built a belief, through different experiences, around the idea that our voices didn't matter. Interestingly, as we shared these stories with each other, we were struck by the similarity in how we both felt we couldn't speak up for our basic human needs for fear of inconveniencing someone else. As adults reflecting on these stories and where these beliefs originated, we are now able to lean into the little girls inside of us with compassion. We can begin to heal these wounds and shift the beliefs from limiting to ones that serve us, from "Our voices and basic needs don't come first" to "Our needs matter, and we get to speak up and use our voices for our needs to be met."

HOW BELIEFS ARE FORMED

How are limiting beliefs formed? And, more importantly, how can we unpack, examine, and disassemble them?

We think about our thinking.

If that sentence just sent your brain into a spin, don't worry! Hang in there with us. Thinking about your thinking is sticky stuff, but when we do, we can unlock the patterns that hold us back.

Our experiences in our early years begin to establish certain beliefs about how the world responds to us. If you have responsive caregivers, you learn that when you are in distress, someone will come to your aid. On the other hand, if your caregivers are inconsistent or disinterested, you may develop a belief that you're on your own and that you must figure out life for yourself.

Our brain craves predictability, so it looks for patterns. We're constantly taking note of how people respond to us and one another. Our notes are compiled into templates that validate what we see. This is called **unconscious patterning**. We are constantly weaving together knowledge and experience to create a better understanding of our world and ourselves. This leads naturally to the creation of beliefs about the world. And as we saw above, those beliefs, when partially or completely false, can actually be detrimental to our success.

We often rode with Grandpa up and down the mountain growing up. On one of those trips, Stacie was seven, and Sandi was five and sitting in the front seat. Grandpa pointed out a sign on the side of the road that said, "Falling Rock."

"Do you know what that sign means?" he asked.

"No," Sandi replied.

"That sign is there because a little boy named Falling Rock went out looking for a bear and got lost. He never came back. His parents put those signs up so that everyone could be on the lookout for Falling Rock," Grandpa said.

Now, anything Grandpa said was absolute truth in our eyes.

From then on, every time Sandi saw the sign that said Falling Rock, she looked for the little boy who got lost in the woods looking for a bear. Now, don't laugh, but it wasn't until Sandi was in college and driving up the mountain to visit friends that she saw the sign and it dawned on her that perhaps the meaning was different. Sandi realized (facepalm moment) that the sign was a warning to motorists that there may be rocks falling from the side of the mountain and littering the roadway. For close to fifteen years, she didn't question what that sign meant.

We don't consciously determine where our beliefs come from at a young age. As we grow, however, we evolve and have the opportunity to examine whether those beliefs are serving us or not. As we reach a place in our lives where we are living with intention, we can make conscious choices about whether we can or want to let go of our beliefs.

Sandi recognized that while Grandpa's story was sweet, it wasn't helping keep her safe from the potential rock striking her car. It was time for her to revisit and shift how she read that sign.

Are you still hanging with us? Let's put another concept into the mix. **Learned behavior** is a close cousin to unconscious patterning. It's a behavior that is not innate but continues to develop into adolescence and adulthood. We begin to learn how to interact with others and to recognize how to connect and build relationships. We're also learning that we may have to shift our behavior depending on the group we're in.

Unconscious patterning and learned behavior contribute to the lens through which we see the world and our place in it. We may begin to shift our behavior depending on the circumstances.

We developed a belief about using—or not using—our voices based upon how our needs were recognized and met in our childhood. It's critical to recognize that no matter what detrimental beliefs you've developed or where they came from, there is no shame in having them. You did nothing wrong, and you aren't damaged goods. You are human. Everyone develops patterns and behaviors. Even the most well-intentioned parents are still humans, carrying their own baggage and unintentionally passing those unhealthy patterns and behaviors on to their children. This unpacking process is one we can all benefit from, no matter how peaceful your upbringing.

While it's important to recognize where our beliefs came from, it is essential not to judge them at this moment. The focus here isn't on whether they are good or bad, right or wrong, but on sussing out if these beliefs are serving you.

ARE YOUR BELIEFS WORKING FOR YOU?

Let's figure out if your beliefs are serving your greater purpose in life. One way to do this is by asking whether the belief is an expanding or limiting belief. An *expanding belief* is one that allows us to open up to all of our capabilities. When our beliefs are expansive, we are able to embrace challenges and grow. *Limiting beliefs* are just as they sound: they keep us penned in. When we're working from a limiting belief, we are not giving ourselves the space to shine.

Our bodies are usually the first to let us know if a belief is expansive or limiting. Sometimes they whisper, and other times they shout. They usually tell us in the form of a visceral sensation. It could be pleasant: you feel happy or peaceful or at ease. This is a sign that a belief is an expansive one; it is working for you—you believe you are loved, you are fulfilled, you are connected.

On the other hand, your body may alert you with an unpleasant sensation when a belief isn't working for you. You may feel uncomfortable or reactive. Perhaps you behave in a way you didn't intend. Maybe you feel anxious, irritated, or alone. When Sandi crouched on the stage in her public speaking class with her face flushed and hot, these sensations were clues that she was dealing with a limiting belief. In that moment, she was in a safe environment, yet her limiting beliefs were getting in the way of her feeling safe.

These uncomfortable sensations are physiological warning signs. It's important to be aware of them because they tell us that a belief has been triggered and core values have been trod upon (we'll talk about core values in Chapter 6). There are instances when the body is giving us useful information before the brain has fully conceptualized the experience.

We often use the terms *feelings and emotions* interchangeably, but they have nuanced meanings. **Emotions** are sparked by sensations in the body, like those physiological signs we mentioned above. They are a natural state of mind, often instigated by a circumstance, mood, or a connection with others.

Feelings are the label we give to the emotions we experience. Our response to the sensation (or emotion) is a feeling. For example, imagine two people standing side by side. Both get a feeling of tightness in their chest and a fluttering in their stomach, and their shoulders rise. One person may say, "I am so anxious," while the other might interpret the feeling as "I'm so excited!"

This often comes up when people talk about stress as though it is coming from outside of themselves. In fact, stress is an internal response. One individual might be sitting in traffic, totally pissed and aggravated. The person in the car in the next lane might be totally relaxed, turning up the music and rocking out. They are both in the same traffic jam, but their response to a circumstance that is entirely out of their control is different.

Another way to understand our patterns and beliefs is to notice the words we use. Pay attention to the language you use when you talk about yourself. What words or phrases appear regularly in your vernacular? Look back through your journal, or even emails or texts. How do you characterize your experiences? Are things happening *to* you? Do you feel as though you have the power and resources to fulfill your potential? If you are working from a limited perspective, you may notice words that imply constraint: *I can't do that. They don't understand. I wish I could have* . . . . Expansive language is open, without boundary, and aspirational. *I am able . . . I am enough . . . I am connected.*

You can also pay attention to the feedback you're receiving in the world. When you are operating from an expansive place, you will likely notice yourself acting and growing in ways you haven't before. Are new opportunities coming your way? Are your relationships deeper and more fulfilling? You are likely in an open, spacious place.

WITNESSING OUR THOUGHTS

Humans have some pretty bizarre thoughts. Our brains go to weird and sometimes disturbing places, and then we think we are unhinged or broken. We are all susceptible to this chaotic brain. It's normal!

When we consider the length of time science has been in existence, the field of neuroscience is barely a blip on the radar. While we've made great strides in learning and understanding the way our gray matter works, it is only a drop in the proverbial bucket of what we have yet to understand.

A number of spiritual traditions suggest observing our thoughts and emotions (as opposed to physiological sensations) as separate from our essence. Sometimes these thoughts and emotions are referred to as the ego. By observing the twisting and turning ways our thoughts move through us, we can begin to cultivate awareness rather than reactivity. This is often referred to as mindfulness.

To practice mindfulness, we simply notice when we are having a thought or an emotion and observe it with curiosity rather than judgment. Where is this thought coming from? How does this thought connect with the feeling I'm having? How is it showing up in my body? By simply drawing attention to these thoughts and sensations without deeming them good or bad, right or wrong, we are taking steps toward unpacking the suitcase we're dragging around.

We sometimes refer to this state of nonjudgmental observation as discerning the difference between our core inner voice (the thoughts that serve us throughout our days), our intuition (the intuitive knowing thoughts that guide us to make helpful choices), or what we jokingly refer to as "the itty-bitty-shitty committee," or backseat driver. You know the type: they always have an opinion or criticism but never offer to take the wheel. The backseat driver is that collection of internal voices we've cultivated over a lifetime that are meant to keep us safe but instead can stunt our growth. It's the voice of fear and judgment. The Backseat Driver is often the voice of limiting beliefs. All these beliefs and narratives that have developed out of fear and judgment get jam-packed into this suitcase. The baggage acts as padding to keep us safe, but it also keeps us small.

What does playing small look like? Playing small is the opposite of showing up as your full self. It is hiding pieces of yourself that could lead to happiness, connection, etc. We play small when self-imposed or perceived judgments are bigger than our authentic self. Playing small is leaning into our limiting beliefs rather than expansive ones. When the "comfort of the familiar" limits our growth, we are playing small.

Imagine a person in a room. Judgment takes up 90 percent of the space between those four walls, leaving the person squeezed into a tiny corner. If all of that judgment is dissolved by acceptance, then the person is able to expand into the space, becoming bigger and more visible. In your own mind, assess the space being taken up by negative self-talk: are you allowing the backseat driver to fill the room?

After we decided to write this book, we each had moments when the old beliefs and stories crept in. The backseat driver was whispering, *"Who do you think you are, writing a book?"* to both of us. The imposter syndrome was REAL!

One day when we were talking about how to actualize this project, Stacie confessed, "What if I don't have anything of value to say? Like, who do I think I am?"

"OMG, me too," Sandi said. She was shocked and touched. It was incredibly reassuring to know that her sister—a person she holds in the highest esteem, who is one of the most capable, intelligent, professional people on the planet—has moments of doubt too! Stacie could feel the tension easing out of her body as Sandi validated her feelings. After all, her confident, savvy, brilliant sister was feeling unsure too.

Rather than let these feelings derail our dream, we were able to remind each other that we can do hard things when we face them together. We stopped, noticed the backseat driver, thanked it for trying to keep us safe, and reminded ourselves that we were at the wheel.

Our clients sometimes ask, "How do you tell the difference between a limiting belief (the backseat driver) and your intuition?" Our best advice is to *practice*.

"Self-awareness is a developmental process," Stacie reminds us. As children, we go through a developmental stage in which we begin to discern how our actions affect others. In a perfect world, as we mature, we begin to listen to our inner knowing, or intuition. Unfortunately, sometimes our upbringing, culture, and social situations instead feed the backseat driver while keeping our intuition quiet. Then, as adults we must undo the work that the backseat driver has done, just as Sandi has been challenged to do in public speaking.

This is a lot of information. Don't worry—you don't have to master thinking about your thinking to keep moving. We can tell you from experience, this is a lifelong practice! The more intentional we are, the more clarity we gain about our place in the world. Remember those three guideposts we talked about in the introduction? Here's where we get to try them out! If you remember to notice, ask questions, and then take the step that feels aligned in the moment, you're on your way down the path to bliss.

KEY NUGGETS:

- ∽ We all develop unconscious patterns and limiting beliefs—it's part of being human.
- ∽ By observing whether a belief is limiting or expansive, we can disrupt the pattern of thinking that holds us back from reaching bliss.
- ∽ We observe beliefs by noticing our physical sensations/visceral reactions and then getting curious about where the belief comes from.

Chapter 2
LENS ON THE WORLD

STACIE: DEVELOPING MY LENS ON THE WORLD

Growing up, I was the odd one out. My Caucasian mother and father of Mexican descent divorced when I was four. I grew up with my mother and two sisters. My mom is blonde, my sisters have fair complexions, and there was me: dark-haired, dark-eyed. It's like I got all Dad's genes and none of Mom's.

As Sandi and I started school, life became even more confusing: I looked Mexican, but my sister looked Caucasian. Big Bear was a predominantly white community, making me feel even more like an outsider.

Sandi had a contradictory experience. Her appearance allowed her to fit in at school—she looked like the rest of the kids in class. But when the last name *Herrera* identified her as Hispanic, she was shuffled into a different box. When we spent weekends with our dad and his family, she looked white and therefore didn't fit in there either.

My youth was often lonely, and I tried to mask it by fitting into every group. I was an athlete, president of SADD (Students Against

Drunk Driving), the school mascot, and a thespian, and I held down a part-time job while excelling in advanced classes. I thought that if I pushed myself into every group and filled my day with activities and tasks, maybe the loneliness would subside. If you saw my room at the time, laundry and papers strewn about my bedroom floor, you would have gotten a glimpse of how I felt inside—disorganized and over-whelmed. I was convinced that if I just kept working and achieving, the accolades and positive feedback would wash the deep sadness away. When that didn't work, I dated a lot, looking for attention from older suitors.

I consistently looked outside of myself for happiness, often saying to myself and others, "I just want to be happy." I didn't have many close friends who knew my whole story. I carried this loneliness into college, not knowing how to simultaneously forge authentic relationships and be seen as the fully capable young woman I knew myself to be. If I kept showing up and meeting others' expectations, maybe I would find my bliss.

In Chapter 1, we talked about how our unconscious patterns and beliefs are formed. My experience as a young Hispanic girl in a predominantly white family and community, and the loneliness and alienation that accompanied that, shaped my patterns and beliefs. Furthermore, it began to shape my lens on the world.

Adolescence is the stage when we begin to seek our community. We start to identify as *I'm like this but not that. I belong here but not there.* Developmentally, it's the time when we are shaping our identity. After spending eighteen years not quite fitting in, by the time I left for college, I had a mission: to find where I belonged.

I believe that my childhood experience of being on the outside of the majority pushed me to develop a sense of wonder about other cultures. I wanted to engage with others, put myself in their shoes, and see the world through their eyes. The lens through which I viewed the world was one of curiosity.

This curiosity led me to study abroad. I spent my junior year in

Tver, Russia, in the early 1990s. Everything you imagine about Russia in the last decade of the twentieth century is true: it was a cold, impoverished nation, yet full of celebration and the highest level of hospitality. For the first two months, I lived in an international dorm with a housemate. We had a kitchen and were expected to prepare our own meals. One day we traipsed down to the local grocery store to replenish our supplies.

"I'd like a dozen eggs, please," I said to the clerk in my very best Russian. The clerk looked at me as though I'd sprouted a second head. I wondered if my Russian was that unintelligible.

If you've ever lived outside the United States, you may recall that everything is sold on a base-ten system; that is, things are sold by the ten, not the dozen. Asking for a dozen eggs was as strange to the store clerk as asking for seven eggs would be in the United States. In this case, my lens on the world was shaped by growing up in the United States. It had never occurred to me that other people and cultures might do basic things differently. Ultimately, it didn't matter whether I got ten or twelve eggs, but I needed to be able to communicate effectively in my new environment. It was time to recalibrate my lens.

While this is a simple example, it helped illuminate this concept for me. I began to consider how my lens might be affecting the other ways I engaged with the world. I recognized that the way I see the world may not be the way others do and that our very different perspectives might impact how we behave. When we are attached to one particular outcome (buying a dozen eggs), we are not open to the possibility of options that are just as good or better (buying ten eggs).

This concept of identifying and evaluating your lens becomes more impactful when you begin to consider other ways you view the world and the belief patterns that are connected to them. For example:

- The world is full of potential pitfalls, so I should be careful (lens of fear).

- I never have enough (lens of scarcity).

∽ People will take advantage of me, so I must be prepared (lens of distrust).

∽ I generalize about a group based upon a bad experience with one (lens of intolerance).

∽ Everyone believes what I believe (lens of naivete).

Many times we don't realize the way our lens is coloring our view and therefore our engagement with the world around us. Recognizing our lens and adjusting it accordingly will drastically shift the way we connect in the world and ultimately influence our overall happiness.

How can you begin to notice and refocus your lens? First, let's talk about the science.

HOW OUR BRAINS WORK

For many years, scientists believed that the brain grew and formed throughout childhood and adolescence. By the time we reached young adulthood in our early to mid-twenties, the brain was cemented and little could be done to shift it. There was no teaching an old (or middle-aged) dog new tricks, as they say.

New research conducted in the last twenty years has proven that this is not the case. Our brains are still malleable all the way through old age. We can continue to learn, shift patterns, and rewire behaviors throughout our lives. Neuroscientists refer to this as ***neuroplasticity***.

Donald Hebb, a Canadian neuropsychologist, coined what is often referred to as Hebb's Rule: "Neurons that fire together, wire together." This principle means that the repeated activation of the same neurons strengthens the connection between them. The more they "fire together," the easier it is to fire in unison again.

Dr. Joe Dispenza, author, chiropractor, and lecturer on neuroscience and quantum physics, refers to this as *hardwiring*, meaning that "If you keep thinking the same thoughts, doing the same things, and feeling the same emotions, you will begin to hardwire your brain into a finite pattern that is the direct reflection of your finite reality."[1] It is as if we become addicted to the patterns we have carved into our brain.

Our brains evolved to be on the lookout for danger and to avoid it at all costs. This was an important survival technique millions of years ago, but these days there are far fewer threats to our immediate safety (more on this in Chapter 3). Still, we are predisposed to watch for potential threats. We are likely to see things through the lens of fear, scarcity, or agitation. As we continue to view the world through our negatively biased lens, we continue to reinforce that neuropathway. Being afraid or angry or experiencing scarcity becomes a habit, even an addiction, which keeps us from living our best, most fulfilled lives.

The good news is that neuroplasticity works both ways. Just as we can strengthen emotions such as anxiety, stress, and anger, we can also cultivate emotions such as happiness, empathy, and abundance.

We could have found ourselves in the habit of viewing ourselves as the odd one out. But we were able to detach from seeing our world in that way and began to open up to new possibilities. We experienced new connections and possibilities after healing from the wounds that left us feeling isolated and alone in our youth. Our whole-person healing journeys included a combination of psychotherapy, integrated healthcare, and spiritual exploration.

READJUSTING YOUR LENS

Let's check back in with the three guideposts of noticing, leading with curious inquiry, and taking aligned action. The following steps are a slightly more nuanced version of those guideposts and will help to readjust the lens we have on the world.

---

1   Dr. Joe Dispenza, *Breaking the Habit of Being Yourself* (Hay House, 2012), 45.

Step 1: Identify and Assess: What is your current lens?

Step 2: Reframing and Refocusing: What kind of lens do you want?

Step 3: Radical Ownership: Understand where the lens came from and shift into "radical ownership."

Step 4: Practice: Activate your imagination. How do you want to feel? Practice.

STEP 1: IDENTIFYING AND ASSESSING

The first step in making any shift in our lives is acknowledging that there is something that needs to change. This is often the most difficult step; most of us don't like to admit that there is something out of alignment. We are afraid that if we admit that we don't like something about ourselves or our behavior, we are "broken." Our society often perceives brokenness as weak. We fight hard to defend our ways of being in the world so we don't have to recognize our own weaknesses.

If we can challenge ourselves to step away from binary thinking (we are either broken or fixed, good or bad, our choices are right or wrong) and invite a more nuanced worldview into our lives, we can begin to make incremental changes. Black and white thinking is a fast track to being overwhelmed—we will talk more about this in Chapter 3. If you believe you are broken, then it is really hard to think about the work involved in getting "fixed." But if you explore the idea that we are all learning and growing, that we need tweaks now and then, adjusting to something new feels more doable.

How do you do this?

Similar to what you did in Chapter 1, start by noticing your language. If you want to shift away from a lens of scarcity, start to notice how you speak about resources. *"There aren't enough hours in the day." "I can't afford that." "I'll never have enough . . ."*

When you notice your thoughts and speech falling into this

pattern, pay attention to how your body responds. How does it feel to check your bank balance? How does your body react when you're given a big task at work? If such a task leads to a feeling of overwhelm or anxiety, the emotional center (amygdala) of your brain is lighting up like a Christmas tree. What does that feel like for you?

STEP 2: REFRAMING AND REFOCUSING

The next step is to recalibrate your lens from how you currently see the world to how you *want* to see the world. Perhaps you've acknowledged that your lens is one of scarcity. Awesome! That's a big step. What are the benefits of having this lens? How does this lens serve you? How does it hold you back? When you can honestly reflect on how your view of the world is working for you, you are seeing the whole picture.

Now, armed with that information, you can get curious: Is this how I want to proceed? Maybe it is! Maybe the safety provided by this view on the world is what you need at this time of your life. Maybe you recognize that you want to tackle reframing it, but there are other more pressing adjustments you're making, so you're going to hold this information lightly and return to it. All these courses of action are perfect.

You might decide that you do, in fact, want to recalibrate this lens. Cool! What sort of lens do you want? Getting specific about what you *do* want is as important as knowing what you want to change. Perhaps you'd like to have a lens of abundance: of having a constantly replenishing reserve of time, energy, and resources at your disposal. You'd like to give freely without resentment or expectation, assuming positive intentions. This is a beautiful acknowledgment of where you want to go.

Have you ever heard the phrase, "Your car goes where your eyes go"? If you have your eye on where the road curves, your body (whether in a car, on a bicycle, or on skis) will naturally turn in that direction. This is why if you are looking off to your left, you'll find yourself swerving that way. By the same token, keeping your eye on the person you aspire to be will help you aim in that direction. This can be hard work—after all, when we've spent our whole lives with a particular mindset, it's often a challenge to imagine what is outside that mindset.

STEP 3: RADICAL OWNERSHIP

Once we've articulated what we want, we take ownership of our actions. What occurred in your life that created the lens through which you see? We unpack the patterns and behaviors that we learned (often in childhood, as we discussed in Chapter 1), and then we realign them. This can feel intense at times! Our goal in this step is to nudge you out of your comfort zone and into your own power. When you can accept how you show up with radical ownership, you are a step closer to authentic bliss.

It is crucial to do this with curiosity, not judgment. When we approach our unpacking from the "I wonder . . ." standpoint, we avoid assigning blame. We step away from binary thinking and recognize that negative behaviors do not make bad people. Shifting our lens asks us to believe that *everyone* is doing the best they can while recognizing that there are consequences for every action.

This is acting with radical ownership. When we accept our circumstances with love and compassion and release resentment and blame, we step into a place of learning and growth. Be gentle with yourself—remember that our brains are predisposed to negativity, and our goal is to lovingly rewire that. We can't rewire ourselves with a positive lens using shame, guilt, and self-inflicted punishment. Shifts in our thinking take time. Ownership is acknowledging where we are in the process of automatic negative thinking as we move toward self-compassion.

STEP 4: PRACTICE

Now that you've identified the lens you want to shift, the way you want to be in the future, and how the lens was created in the first place, let's start to make that change.

"How?" you ask. Practice.

Now that you've begun to notice your patterns and your body's response to them, you can begin to retrain them. When you feel your stomach drop as the bill comes at dinner, notice it. Is there a legitimate reason? More than likely, you decided to go to dinner knowing you had the funds to cover it. Remind yourself that you have enough.

But perhaps even more importantly, imagine what it feels like when you have enough money, time, and love in your life. What does it feel like when you get a raise or an unexpected gift or have a free day off? Do you feel free, unencumbered, and joyous? Perhaps you feel full of gratitude and buoyant. Remember this feeling and practice it. Taking time to journal or recount moments of joy or gratitude will increase overall feelings of happiness and contentment. Remember, neurons that fire together wire together. You are creating a new path of joy and abundance for your brain to use.

SANDI: FINDING MY AUTHENTIC LENS

I have spent my entire life moving and chasing what's next, what's better, what's more, so learning to slow down long enough to readjust this lens has taken *a lot* of work.

I have often shared the story of moving eight times in the sixteen years of growing up in Big Bear. My story is always laced with a tone of ambivalence that I now know was masking the feeling of never being settled, never truly feeling grounded, of seeking a safe place to come home to when life gets tough. My search comes out of this deep longing to be able to count on someone, someplace. When Stacie and I are together, I feel that security. But I don't want her to feel as though she has to take care of me, even though I know that's what she loves to do. I feel this need to protect her from having to do so.

Our childhood "on the move" stemmed from our mom doing the best she could, based on her income or lack thereof. When Mom had money, we moved to nicer places. When funds were low, we had to move again. We got really good at packing and resettling all the time. Our moves were like a real-life game of Tetris, and I got very good at packing a lot into a little space.

While I built a lot of resilience with the consistent uncertainty of where we would have to move next, the shadow side of all this moving around is that I never truly felt settled and was always seeking what was next in an attempt to normalize our transient lifestyle. The under-current of fear that is rooted in the lack of stability has carried into my adult life and shown up in my own limiting money beliefs and a lens on the world of feeling like the rug could be pulled out from under me at any moment.

Once I moved into my dorm at California Lutheran University, the moves that happened each break and each school year felt easy and normal to me. When I graduated, Stacie was coming home from living in Russia for a year teaching English, and we decided to move into a fantastic little beach apartment together in Port Hueneme, California. Because my sense of "home" and safety was always anchored in my connection with my sister, *this* move felt like a coming home and so easy and natural . . . I'd arrived!

Despite my programmed level of comfort with living in constant transition, I still had this deeply rooted, unconscious belief that life was supposed to involve a house surrounded by a white picket fence, being rescued by a man who would take care of everything and "save me" from ever being harmed. I call this my "Cinderella Story" or the "White Picket Fence Plan." When Stacie moved on to follow her Cinderella Story, it was naturally my time to do the same (that's what little sisters do, right?!).

So I nudged my boyfriend toward the next step in the White Picket Fence Plan, and we found our home to begin this dream life I thought I was supposed to live. It was all going according to plan, or at least someone's plan. What I didn't know or trust at the time was that I wasn't living my story, the life meant for me . . . I was living the life that was expected of me.

Once we decided to get married (since that's obviously the next logical step in life—graduate high school, graduate college, find love, move in together, get married, have 2.5 kids, and build the white picket fence), we moved to Vegas to be closer to his family and for him to have a job that didn't involve travel. Check the next box on the Cinderella Story to-do list.

Side note: right before walking down the aisle, my dad said to me, "It's not too late if you don't want to," and my obligatory good girl self laughed it off and said, "Nope, I'm ready," without a second thought or check-in with myself.

In 2001, after two and a half years of an emotional and painful infertility journey and three heartbreaking miscarriages, our son Hunter was born on my birthday. Thank goodness . . . White Picket Fence Plan complete. Now, live happily ever after . . . or so I thought since I was following the script that all the princess stories had taught me, none of which involved learning to trust what I wanted and what I needed.

Mind you, I don't regret getting married for all the lessons and blessings it has brought to my life. I simply never learned to listen to my truest self, my intuition, and design a life through the lens of the most authentic version of myself.

In the twenty-five years living in Vegas, my moves included:

1. Our first home, the place I was carried across the threshold, the home where we brought our newborn baby

2. The home that was zoned for the best schools

3. The house with a pool: after all, our son has lots of friends

4. The big "forever" home, with all the things we are supposed to have: the dedicated home office, the loft/playroom, the big garage, the guest suite, the big yard . . .

5. My little house to heal after my divorce

6. Another big house to try the fairytale again

7. The first home I bought all for me, where Hunter and I would build our lives from a solid foundation

8. . . . and now . . . well, I'll get to that in Chapter 3.

You can probably see this pattern repeating itself. The pattern creates a lens that says, "Moving is normal." It tells me it's "safer" to not stay in one place because that's what my nervous system has been taught since childhood. Our brains and bodies like the familiar and normalize what is known versus what may or may not be healthy for us.

Once I noticed this pattern, which honestly took until house #7 from above *(some lenses on the world are slow to reveal themselves to us when they can be obvious to those who love us),* I was able to get curious and take aligned action. My curiosity led me down a path of unpacking the layers of neuropathways that led to this unconscious lens on the world telling me it was safer to always be looking for what's next, versus the lens I have today, which is to be present to all the gifts that are right in front of me. I spent several years in intense discovery with a variety of practitioners, doctors, and therapists to navigate this and several other pieces of my journey. And I continue to explore and unpack my beliefs and lenses through which I look at the world, all with the intention of living a life open to all possibilities and an open mind and heart to learning what I may not yet be able to see through my current lens on the world.

KEY NUGGETS:

We are learning about how the brain works—and how we can re-wire it using the following steps:

Step 1: Identify what your current lens is (noticing).

Step 2: What lens do you want (recalibrating)?

Step 3: Understand where the lens came from but shift into "radical ownership."

Step 4: Activate your imagination: How do you want to feel? Practice.

Chapter 3
THINKING ON PURPOSE

SANDI: DESIGNING MY LIFE ON PURPOSE

It's two o'clock in the afternoon on a Wednesday in January 2023, and I'm sitting in a coffee shop in the Hallmark movie-esque New England town of Portsmouth, New Hampshire. This is my first experience in the life I've always dreamed of, and it feels unnatural and surreal. And yet I know with my entire self that this is where I am meant to be. I feel an unwavering embodiment of peace and alignment from all the choices and experiences that have led me here.

Just one year prior, I was visiting Florida for work and family time. I had been talking about moving out of Vegas for *years* and dreaming of living at the beach again like Stacie and I had done right after college. I had been avoiding actually doing something about it because my maternal instincts kept telling me that Hunter needed me (even though he was now a self-sufficient young adult) . . . and because I had just bought my beautiful home in Vegas . . . and because I didn't know if I could afford it . . . and because what if it didn't work out . . . and because, because, because . . .

I walked into Stacie's kitchen one evening and started looking through the pantry for a snack. She was sitting at the kitchen table working on something on her laptop.

"So, Sand . . . there are beaches on the East Coast too," Stacie said. Then, thinking of her daughter, she added, "Sabina knows of yoga studios in Virginia Beach you might like."

"Mmmhmmm," I responded.

"Let's call Sabina and see; let's land the plane. We can connect you with people who live there and know about these places to help you either rule it in or rule it out." Stacie was off and running. She started asking me questions, even though I was simply looking for a snack. True to her sisterly intuition, she knew I needed a nudge to get me out of my own way.

As her questions proceeded, I was hooked into articulating the dream of where I truly desired to live. Next thing you know, I'm sitting next to her with both our computers open and Sabina and Katie (my niece and her friend) on FaceTime adding more ideas and invigorating questions to the conversation!

All I knew before this beautiful inquisition was that it was time to build my life for me now that I was about to be a midlife, single, empty nester, and no one was going to build this life that I dreamt of for me. I was going to have to figure it out if I was truly going to find MY bliss. I had been "nose to the grindstone" since 2010, working as an entrepreneur and a single mom, growing my business to a place where I can travel to see my clients when I am not working with them remotely. The path to realizing my authentic dream life was filled with many fetal-position moments, praying for God to help me pay the rent so I could keep doing this work, and one too many times having to rack up my credit cards to make ends meet.

All I knew was that I wanted to live at the beach, and while I loved my community in Vegas, it was time for a change. Since I was raised in Southern California, went to college there, and chose the beach right after college, a So Cal beach was the obvious choice to me and everyone who knew me. Stacie helped me give myself permission to dive into the experiences I wanted to have, the things I wanted to feel, and the types of people I wanted to build a community with. I dreamed of a place on the ocean and was open to any ocean. I wanted a place where I could walk to a yoga studio, juice bar, and local coffee shop. I wanted to be able to take a day trip to ski in the winter and walk the beach in the summer (and winter too, because I love a quiet, cold, beach walk). I wanted hiking and nature and a slow, mindful pace. I wanted a community of friendly neighbors who show up for each other through celebrations and lean on each other in times of need.

After three hours, I had a list of cities to "date" and a dream of what life could look like for REAL and for ME. My new empty nester life was about to begin!

Now, I was packed for the warmth of Florida in January since that was my only planned destination. I had a list of cities in the Northeast that I was excited to explore, but I didn't exactly have the ideal clothing to weather January in that part of the country. I was ready to fly home to Vegas and think about postponing the plan to "city-date" for the future.

"Why don't you just go now?" Stacie asked. "Change your flight. Why not?"

Obviously, I had a million reasons why I couldn't just go to New England right now. *I have work to do. It's expensive to change my flight, let alone the cost of places to stay and car rentals. I'm definitely not packed for New England winters.* Stacie pulled a hat, scarf, and set of boots out of her closet to prepare me for my journey. She wasn't going to let me avoid my fate. Despite the fact that she keeps hope alive that someday I'll move to Florida and into the house next door, she was ready to support my journey wherever I landed.

My city-dating adventure took me through six cities in the first week and then another five over the next three months, not to mention the countless virtual dates I went on with cities all over the world. For the first time in my life, I gave myself permission to design my entire life ON PURPOSE.

As I explored each city, I gave myself permission to challenge my deeply rooted beliefs, opened my imagination to what could be, led with the curiosity of a new traveler, and took aligned actions with whatever my intuition was saying. I was able to experience the culture of what it was like to live there, by learning to listen to weird intuitive pulls.

You know those little nudges that happen when you're driving on the freeway, and you know you need to go around someone, and then the freeway opens up with a wide-open lane for you to drive at your own pace? Or when you have an inkling to stop by a certain coffee shop and then you run into a friend you haven't seen in years, and they say something you needed to hear? I was letting my heart be wide-open to those intuitive pulls throughout my city-dating experience. Through those intuitive nudges, I knew I'd be led to the right spot to land.

After spending a beautiful day in Virginia Beach, I stayed at a gorgeous bed-and-breakfast in Cape Charles, Virginia, a tiny community just off the coast. The owner suggested a couple of options for dinner. After watching the wildly colorful sunset from my balcony, I drove into the little town and decided to have dinner at Kelly's Pub. What better way to learn about the town than from the local bartender? He was a friendly man who shared stories of beautiful people connected in community and politely asked me to lunch the next day. I texted my girlfriends jokingly, "Did I just teleport into a Hallmark movie?" It was just the type of spontaneous opportunity I was open to in order to truly learn what it was like to live in Cape Charles, named the "Best Beach Town in Virginia." I had a wonderful time, and the scenery was gorgeous, but it wasn't for me.

While in Newport, Rhode Island, I decided to take one of my virtual meetings from a fabulous vegan restaurant. When I wrapped up, I wasn't ready to retreat to my Airbnb yet, so I let my intuition guide me into an Italian restaurant two doors down for my last meeting of the day. I met a group of older gentlemen sitting next to my table who were having a very inspiring conversation about mental health that led me to interrupt and introduce myself. An hour later, I had new friends who said if I chose Newport, I should feel free to meet them back there any Thursday night.

I left the restaurant feeling incredibly grateful for the easy sense of community. While I was feeling as though my cup was full to the brim, I still wasn't ready to call it a night. A few doors down was a local pub, Pour Judgement (obviously I needed to go in). The place was super crowded, filled with a fun, inviting energy, and I found a seat at the bar. Funny enough, the bartender knew someone I went to high school with. I loved the sense of community I found in Newport, but it still didn't feel quite right.

After I shared my city-dating adventures on social media, another friend from high school reached out and said, "Hey, you're in my neck of the woods. Where are you heading to next?"

Unfortunately, I had to shift my plans. A nor'easter storm kept me in Newport for a few extra days, meaning I didn't get to the last city I was hoping to see, Newburyport, Massachusetts. I shared with my friend that I was flying out from Boston and had time for dinner if it worked for him. We had such a great time catching up! I loved learning about his family and how they had settled in Portsmouth, New Hampshire, and why they loved it. I promised I would come back soon and have one more city-dating experience in New England.

The evening I arrived in Portsmouth in March 2022, I got settled into my Airbnb and woke up the next day to a morning full of virtual meetings. I'd planned to head out for an afternoon of exploring after I finished my last call. As we were wrapping up, I looked up and noticed a beautiful, light snow falling, and my heart leapt with childlike excitement.

"I've gotta go," I told my colleagues. "It's snowing, and I gotta go out and play!"

I had collected an immense amount of information through my city-dating extravaganza. It was time to get quiet with myself. I didn't do the normal make-a-list, write-out-pros-and-cons (while that does serve me sometimes, this was not one of those times). I knew with every part of me that I needed to make this choice without my logical mind but instead with a deeply rooted amount of intuition and self-trust.

I chose to move to a place I didn't even know existed before January 2022: Portsmouth, New Hampshire. It has felt like home since the moment I first visited that March.

Each moment throughout that first trip and each trip for the rest of the year was infused with excitement to just BE in this place. With each new restaurant and each new person I met, I thought to myself, "I get to live here!"

I had finally made a choice for ME, by my design. I can make the list of all the "reasons" I moved here, but the most important one is that it just feels right and aligned with my life story, my values, and where I am meant to begin this next book of my life. I've closed the first one with love and gratitude for all of the experiences, lessons, and amazing humans whom I get to call friends and family. I am carrying forward so much and also feel like Bambi learning to walk for the first time.

This traveler's journey is never complete; there is no arrival . . . only stops along the way to catch your breath, soak it all in or exhale and let it all go. Either way, when you begin to live it on purpose, trusting your unique intuitive wisdom, your blissful path truly comes alive in ways you once only thought existed in your dreams.

PACKING YOUR SUITCASE

Do you have the proper gear for this journey, or are you carrying around more than you need? Let's take a look:

- ᔈ Do you believe you have to control the future to be successful?
- ᔈ Does your mind automatically see everything that could go wrong without recognizing everything that could go right?
- ᔈ Do you only see one path to the desired outcome?

If any of these questions resonate with you, you might fall into a rigid thinking trap. Rigid thinking can often make navigating the path to unpacking bliss quite challenging.

What Is Rigid Thinking?

In order to understand rigid thinking, we have to first understand how our brains have evolved. In Chapter 2, we discussed our evolutionary wiring to negativity bias and began to explore the ways to use the neuroplasticity of our brains to rewire our thinking. Let's explore that a little deeper.

At the dawn of time, our ancestors had to contend with all sorts of threats that we no longer have to worry about: untreatable disease, predators, etc. Our caveman brain was designed to be on the lookout for potential threats.

In *Hardwiring Happiness,* neuropsychologist Rick Hanson explains that humans evolved to propagate the species by pursuing pleasure or "carrots" (shelter, food, sex) and avoiding pain or "sticks" (starvation, predators, aggression). Both were important, but "sticks have more urgency than carrots. If you fail to get a carrot today, you'll have another chance to get one tomorrow, but if you fail to avoid a stick today . . . no more carrots forever."[2]

As a result, our brains evolved to be on the lookout for the sticks, or "negativity bias." We pay more attention to the negative threats because our brains are wired to perceive negative stimuli more easily and quickly than positive stimuli. One of the areas of your brain circuitry that is responsive to these stimuli is the amygdala, which is responsible for the more widely known "fight-flight-freeze-or-fawn" response. When your amygdala senses danger, it triggers these reactions. In prehistoric times, this might have looked like literally running away, or battling the invader, or playing dead. Today, however, our responses look a little different:

---

2   Rick Hanson, PhD, *Hardwiring Happiness: The New Brain Science of Contentment, Calm, and Confidence* (Harmony Books, 2016), 20.

Fight: You may notice yourself becoming more argumentative, defensive, or frustrated. You may notice your jaw clench, the urge to stomp or kick, or a churning in your gut.

Flight: This may show up as becoming anxious or fidgety or a general feeling of restlessness. You may find yourself redirecting conversations away from things that are uncomfortable or unfamiliar to you.

Freeze: When we are overcome with the freeze impulse, we are in a state of overwhelm. We might disengage from our surroundings. You may feel a sense of dread, your heart may be pounding, or you may feel heavy or numb. You may appear unresponsive or frozen to others.

Fawn: This concept is one that is newer to many of us. It suggests that a response to danger is to become compliant or agreeable to deflect, similar to the concept of Stockholm Syndrome, where a captive feels compassion for their kidnapper.[3]

Negativity bias also reveals the universal reaction where we dwell on one bad event that occurred during the day and allow it to sweep us into a long-lasting negative mood, even if twenty good events also happened during that day. This propensity to negativity bias often leads us to unhealthy thinking patterns, such as:

Binary Thinking: Thinking in black and white, either/or, not recognizing the shades of gray or nuance. Sometimes referred to as "all or nothing thinking."

Disqualifying the Positive: Ignoring the good things you've done or accomplished or suggesting that they are insignificant.

Catastrophizing: Thinking of the absolute worst things that can happen.

---

3   Pete Walker, "Codependency, Trauma and the Fawn Response," *The East Bay Therapist*, Jan/Feb 2003, https://pete-walker.com/codependencyFawnResponse.htm.

Tunnel Vision: Focusing on only one way forward without consideration of alternatives.

Focusing on the Outcome: Placing importance on the end result without consideration for the journey itself.

Does any of this sound familiar? We both find ourselves in these patterns from time to time. We are most often derailed by catastrophic thinking. Stacie could have gotten a gold medal in catastrophizing when she thought about her children studying abroad during the pandemic. When Sandi was a new mom, like lots of new parents out there, she watched Hunter sleep to make sure he was still breathing. *Is he breathing too fast? Too slow?* She would reassure herself that he was fine and go back to bed, and then, just as she was getting comfortable, her eyes would pop open. *Oh my god, what if he's stopped breathing now??* Sandi would jump out of bed and go back to check on him again.

Whether you are a parent or caregiver or not, you can probably recognize the pattern. You are fine, and then something happens, and you start to think about all the potential disasters that could happen, and before you know it, you have fallen down a rabbit hole of catastrophic thinking. We are human, and this is normal. We are never going to completely eradicate this tendency, but we can begin to catch it earlier and lovingly readjust.

When we notice ourselves falling into these patterns, the trick is to do as Rick Hanson suggests and rewire that neuropathway. The good news is that our brains are incredibly malleable. Research over the past several decades shows that our brains can continue to learn and adapt to changes until we die—this is great news! We just have to carve a different path.

We like to characterize this as Thinking On Purpose: the act of reframing our thoughts in a way that aligns with our values, desires, and strengths. We get to reform our thoughts; that way we control them, not the other way around.

FORGING A NEW (NEURO) PATHWAY

We've spent a lot of time observing our thoughts and behaviors in the last couple chapters. Now that you have some practice, you are likely able to note when you've fallen into a fight/flight/freeze/fawn state.

Once again, we return to our three guideposts: observing, curious inquiry, and aligned action. The first step to healing is to notice your bodily sensations, your thoughts, and your behaviors. As you become more familiar with those feelings, you might note what is happening in your body when you find yourself suddenly defensive or disengaged. Note where your nervous system is lighting up. This might feel like a quickening of your breathing or like your shoulders are up near your ears. You might feel a change in your body temperature, either quite warm or a chill. You may be labeling this as fear, anxiety, anger, or even boredom.

When you become aware of these things—you guessed it—get curious (our second guidepost). What is causing this response? When you notice that you are fidgeting or disconnecting from your reality during a tough conversation, you can begin to approach yourself from a place of kind, compassionate curiosity. *What is going on for me at this moment?* Gently remind yourself that you are not broken; there is nothing wrong with you. *Why am I feeling this triggered sensation right now? How can I lovingly care for myself and restore my equilibrium?* From that place of knowledge, you can take the next step (our third guidepost): aligned action.

When you consider your next step, try letting go of moving toward an outcome. Most of our society is heavily focused on product rather than process. We've found the hyper-fixation on outcomes to be less fulfilling at best and damaging at worst. As we've discussed, the path we are on doesn't have an endpoint. We are simply refining and reworking our ways of being in the world; there is no arrival. Rather than being focused on a goal, a new way of embracing your journey is to center on how you feel.

In *The Desire Map: A Guide to Creating Goals with Soul*, Danielle LaPorte tells us, "When you get clear on how you want to feel, the pursuit itself will become more satisfying."[4] In order to sidestep our hardwired negativity bias, we should ask ourselves the simple question:

How do I want to feel?

When we focus on the desired feeling, we begin the process of thinking on purpose. We give space for a multitude of paths or outcomes. This releases the expansive process of **quantum thinking**. Quantum thinking allows us to believe all things are possible and interconnected. Where binary thinking is black and white, this or that, quantum thinking invites us into the infinite shades and hues in between. When we find ourselves in quantum thinking, we are more comfortable with nuance. We trust that the universe may have beautiful paths in mind for us that we can't even begin to imagine! When you change the way you think, you begin to change your life.

Quantum thinking allows us to believe that there are infinite possibilities unique to our soul's purpose on this planet. It is by definition expansive! When we are thinking on purpose, we are in quantum thinking, and the possibilities are endless.

Quantum thinking is a topic that deserves a book all its own—and in fact, many have been written about this concept. We are early in our own journey and exploration to hold multiple perspectives and opposing thoughts in mind. For us, quantum thinking pulls us out of the details of life that can feel heavy and reminds us that life can be challenging and simultaneously exhilarating. We won't detour down this side road too far, but feel free to explore this topic on your own.

STACIE: THINKING BIG

I was a first-generation college student. When I was in college, there wasn't much guidance about how to choose a major. You major

---

4   Danielle LaPorte, *The Desire Map: A Guide to Creating Goals with Soul* (Sounds True, 2014).

in what you like, so I studied anthropology and Russian studies, and as I shared earlier, I spent a year in Russia my junior year. That's where I met my first husband. After graduation, I struggled to find work. I thought I wanted to be a teacher. After all, I spent a lot of years working with younger children. I remember being an older elementary student and being sent to kindergarten classrooms to help younger students. That's how early on I was identified as someone who worked well with young people, and I really wanted to be in a teacher role.

I quickly learned that if you don't have the skills for classroom management, you are going to struggle in a teaching position. I wanted to work with kids one-on-one, but I didn't know how to do that. Life happens, and I eventually found work as an executive assistant and an office manager. After the birth of my third child, we moved to Florida to be closer to my husband's family, and I was lucky enough to have five and a half years to be a stay-at-home mom. Because really, the cost of childcare would have eaten up my entire salary, as the jobs I had didn't pay much. It was a beautiful opportunity to really bond with my children.

As Amelia, my youngest daughter, entered kindergarten, I recognized that I needed to do something. I didn't want to go back to work as an office manager for a variety of reasons, namely because it didn't pay well. I was adrift.

I started exploring. I asked myself: *What really lights me up? How do I want to spend my days? What makes me feel good?* I thought back to my undergraduate degree and the time I spent studying second language acquisition. I was very invested in understanding how people learn. I'd always liked working with young people, but I knew the classroom wasn't the right place for me. I started investigating educational psychology programs. Lo and behold, there just happened to be a school psychology program nearby.

I went in to talk with the school psychologist who evaluated my oldest daughter when she was selected for the gifted program. I wanted to better understand what this whole school psychology thing was all about.

"Well, it's a lot of working with students one-on-one, understanding unique ways of learning, and teaching others about how students will learn," he said. *Oh, I like that a lot*, I thought. "And it's using assessment and numbers to evaluate students." I could feel my excitement rising. I was good with systems and analytics. *Oh, this could be a really fascinating profession.*

The school psychology program I found was a blended program, which meant that it was partially online and partially in person. As a stay-at-home mom who was still having to juggle all the things, it felt like a really good fit. There were some drawbacks, though. It was a small, for-profit university. The program was very expensive, so I had to take out a number of loans. At the time, paying out of pocket for over $1,000 per credit hour just wasn't possible. Because the school was small, I knew I would have to get really good at finding my own learning opportunities. It was a huge leap of faith. But I got really good at advocating for my needs and figuring things out on the fly, and I'm better for it.

Grad school was simultaneously (in my mind) an audacious leap (who am I to pursue a doctorate?) and terrifying. Was it truly my life's purpose or another attempt at meeting others' expectations? My maternal grandmother and a dear family friend had each commented on how they had thought I would amount to more, make a bigger impact than working in an office or being a stay-at-home mom. Their words were a spark and a sting, knowing I had failed to meet their expectations. Would grad school fill that void? Would it provide me with the financial freedom I craved? Would I live up to my own expectations of making a big impact in the world? My self-confidence was very low when I began my graduate program. If you asked others, they'd say they didn't notice, mostly because I have mastered the art of only showing feelings people expect to see and hiding other feelings; always looking calm, cool, and collected. Learning to trust myself and others with my feelings came much later in my story.

I did a lot of things to get by financially. I cleaned houses; I painted faces at children's birthday parties. I also took advantage of lots of learning opportunities along the way. I asked to go to different conferences and made sure I had all of the books that were on the syllabi, not just the required ones. Still, I worried that maybe I didn't belong there; there was no GRE requirement to get in, so I had to stare down my own issues with imposter syndrome. I remember talking with Sandi about whether I should stop with a master's degree or continue to finish the doctorate. Always my biggest cheerleader, Sandi helped me weigh the options, and when it was clear that the doctorate was the best fit for me, she was in celebration mode.

"Hell, yeah, you're getting your PhD!" she cheered. In reality, I received a doctorate in school psychology, which is a PsyD, but that's just splitting hairs.

I did two years of internship in Sarasota County, and then at the end of my second year of internship, I was faced with another leap of faith moment. The lead school psychologist (the same one I'd talked to before starting the program) called me into his office and told me they didn't have a job opening for me.

"Okay," I said calmly. He looked at me, a little surprised.

"Are you sure? You're taking this rather well," he said, looking dumbfounded. I shrugged. I had a sense that there would be something better out there.

The thing was, I was starting to open myself up to new ways of thinking. A lot of healing occurred during my graduate studies after my divorce. It was just great timing, although that's not what I would have said at the time. Going through a divorce while attending graduate school to become a psychologist provided a unique support system. As part of the program, we were encouraged to seek out our own therapeutic support, in addition to the coursework that required consistent self-reflection. The path was painful. Physically, I dropped a considerable amount of weight and began experiencing debilitating migraines while grappling with the stress and anxiety of recognizing that my marriage was no longer healthy, and I needed to make a significant change in my life.

Prior to graduate school, I had been a stay-at-home mom for several years. The financial implications of divorce were severe, yet the rewards of no longer being in an unhealthy relationship outweighed the financial security of the marriage. Completing my doctoral degree and internship while living on the equivalent of substitute bus driver pay was challenging and would have been impossible without the loving support of my family, community, friends, and colleagues. Between studying different modalities through my program and my own spiritual path, I'd begun to open up to more positive psychology, so I was able to believe that there was some sense to the chaos. I knew this was my purpose on this planet. I trusted that intuition, and I knew that the best outcome would reveal itself.

I interviewed for a job in the next county to the north but didn't really want to commute. I chatted with a local clinical psychologist who specializes in working with children. She was hesitant about the prospect of hiring me for a postdoctoral position but wanted to be helpful. It was a unique opportunity and set me on the path to doing what I do now. If I hadn't started working for her, I would have stayed in the school system doing school psychology. But instead, I became interested in private practice and eventually opened my own and later a second company.

The way I see it now, I have so much more impact doing this work in this manner. My practice serves children and families, and it provides school-based mental health opportunities as well. We are able to deliver interventions and build toward ongoing growth with our clients, as opposed to being limited to a few minutes per student and trying to train educators to deliver interventions. It was a big, scary leap into a very uncertain space, but what we've built is making a profound ripple in our community.

Maybe it would have been easier to just find an office job while my kids were in school and not enter into a graduate degree program. Maybe it would have been easier to take a job as a school psychologist in a school district and not leap into private practice. But if there's an easy path out there, I have not always taken it. I knew that I was interested in learning more and trying something new. I allowed myself to let go of the outcome and stay with the feeling that I wanted as opposed to being fixated on a particular goal, and my attempt at quantum thinking paid off. Making an impact, being content and aligned with my values, using my talents, and creating meaningful connections became my North Star.

A NOTE ON JUDGMENT

Part of this process is acknowledging our progress *and* not judging our past selves. Rather than beating ourselves with the "shame bat" over what we *should* have done, we choose love instead. It doesn't do anyone any good to look back over our journey of personal growth and be critical of the way we acted, reacted, made decisions, or forged relationships in the past.

We don't know what we don't know until we know we don't know.

Which leads to another important point, we have to believe that change is possible. As humans, we are emotional beings, yet if we believe that some emotions are bad and should remain hidden or never discussed, it will be challenging to change our responses. Recent research conducted by Dr. James J. Gross indicates that there's a key connection between beliefs about the controllability of emotions and the use of emotional regulation strategies.[5] The more we view all emotions as signals that are more helpful than harmful, the easier it is to navigate the windy roads of our emotional responses. The first step may be

---

5   This concept is central to the work of James J. Gross, particularly his research on emotion regulation and its underlying mechanisms. See, for example, Gross (2014)

recognizing that uncomfortable feelings may arise from the emotions we experience, and our behavior may reflect our discomfort. Your belief about these emotions will drive your ability to change your behavior and how you are feeling.

Life is a process. We all have unhealthy patterns that we want to replace. The important bit is that we make the choice to restructure and rewire. Part of restructuring is to be compassionate with our former selves. And guess what? We're always evolving, learning, and growing. There's no end to this journey; we are dynamic beings. As we like to say, "It's about practice, not perfection." If we instead approach our life through a lens of learning, we are more able to flex our thinking and make changes.

Allowing ourselves to love our imperfect selves in all our marvelous iterations marks the shift from *rigid thinking* to *quantum thinking*.

What's more, when we are able to love our imperfect, emotional selves, both past and present, we are teaching our brains to be kind and compassionate to other humans as well. We can hold ourselves and others accountable while still being loving and empathetic with the stumbles and falls.

KEY NUGGETS

- ᔆ We can rewire our brains from rigid thinking to quantum thinking.
- ᔆ Rigid thinking is how our brains have evolved over time. We fall into instinctual fight/flight/freeze/fawn patterns.
- ᔆ We can rewire this and learn to think more expansively by letting go of outcomes and focusing on how we want to *feel*.

Chapter 4

THE PLAYGROUND OF PERMISSION

PLAY WITH PERMISSION

You've packed your suitcase, adjusted your mirrors, and are ready to focus on the journey ahead, not the destination. Before you embark on your traveler's adventure, we invite you to pause and play with the idea of giving yourself permission. In this chapter, we're going to work through what we call the *Playground of Permission*. The first step is to give yourself permission to simply *be*.

Permission is a pretty simple concept: you are allowing yourself to be as you are and feel exactly what you are feeling in the moment. There are numerous ways to do this, and we'd suggest dabbling in them all to see what gives you a sense of ease. This journey of unpacking our bliss can sometimes feel challenging—we're digging into old stories, examining our beliefs and history, and that can be heavy. But there are opportunities to lightly dance and play with new ways of being too. We like to think of this portion of the journey as a chance to welcome a sense of childlike wonder into the process.

STACIE: I GIVE MYSELF PERMISSION TO LOVE IMPERFECTLY

Roland and I had known each other for years and had been dating for six months. We had four children between us, and they were a very important part of our relationship. The children were very comfortable with us being together, so when Roland decided to propose to me, he wanted them to be involved in the process.

One evening, we loaded all six of us into the minivan and headed to the nearby Olive Garden. Little did I know what my partner had up his sleeve! He'd plotted a proposal—family style.

Roland wanted each of the children to touch the ring before he popped the question. The kids ranged in age from nine to twelve, so you can imagine the chaos that ensued as they tried to secretly pass this ring around the table without me noticing. The boys marched off to the bathroom, and when they returned, they were holding something. I was certain they'd picked something up in the men's restroom.

"Boys, whatever you two have picked up in there, go throw it away. Go wash your hands. We don't pick things up off the bathroom floor. That's gross," I said, exasperated.

Meanwhile, Roland began to say things. He was waxing on nervously about how things had been going great, and I started to feel uneasy. My catastrophic brain began to panic. *Oh my god, he's breaking up with me. Why else would anyone say things like this again and again unless they are leading up to bad news?*

My soon-to-be stepson must have noticed my panicked look and said, "It's good; you'll like it." When I finally realized Roland was actually asking me to marry him, my panic faded, but the uneasiness remained. *Why do we need to do this?* I thought. *I am perfectly comfortable just living together. Why do we need to formalize this thing?* But I loved him, of course, and I loved our life together.

"Yes, okay," I said.

When we got home, I slipped into the bedroom, into his closet, and started to cry. When he found me there, weeping under his dress shirts, he looked at me, puzzled.

"I'm no good at marriage," I blurted. Both of my parents have been married three times, and I desperately wanted to break the cycle of unhealthy relationships. I stayed in my first marriage despite the fact that we were both deeply unhappy. I didn't want to try again without some assurance that I could do better, that I had worked on my behaviors and communication patterns enough to contribute effectively to a committed relationship. I was scared of not doing it "the right way." The truth is, though, I'd never have proof that I could succeed without trying, and I knew that too.

Roland wasn't fazed by my reaction. He wasn't hurt that I was responding to his gesture of profound love and commitment with tears and fear. He simply hugged me.

"You just haven't been married to the right person," he said.

I learned in that moment that I had permission to feel however I was feeling, and this man would love and accept me. This lesson took several months of practice to become an automatic thought. I didn't have to feel guilty about responding to his loving gesture of commitment with fear. I didn't have to put his needs before my own. I could simply feel what I felt in the moment. In fact, it was okay for me to feel multiple emotions at once—trepidation and panic on one hand and love and safety on the other.

I had to unpack the fact that I was raised not to be a burden. I learned early on not to ask for help. In my first marriage, I trained myself to put my husband's comfort before my own needs. What's more, I was rewarded for doing so. Everyone admired how strong and capable I was, and that validation continued to reinforce my belief that I had to handle everything without asking for help or addressing my own needs. I wasn't able to give myself permission to feel—much less articulate—what I needed. I was doing my best when everyone else's needs were met. It was completely unfamiliar to slow down and ask for what

I needed before ensuring everyone around me had been supported.

It took a long time for me to give myself permission to ask for what I needed and to feel my feelings. When I was able to allow myself to address my needs and feel my emotions, I could then decide what boundaries I needed to have in place to take care of myself. I've learned that there is a tremendous amount of power in this. By allowing your feelings to simply be, you are also creating space for others to do the same. Modeling this for those around me, especially my children, is important to increasing emotional intelligence and creating psychologically safe spaces.

FEEL IT TO HEAL IT

You woke up late and found the dog used your favorite flats as a chew toy. The kids bickered over the cereal choices all through breakfast. The middle child informed you they need poster paper for a project that is due later in the day. Traffic was a nightmare, and as you pulled away from the drop-off lane, some jerk cut you off and nearly caused an accident. You look down at the steering wheel and realize you've been gripping it so hard your knuckles are white, and all you want to do is scream.

Does this sound familiar? That kind of morning will set anyone's teeth on edge! And feeling like you are about to burst is a completely natural and human reaction to a bevy of chaotic, frustrating occurrences all in a row. Your irritation, frustration, *even rage* are completely okay.

Just one more time: *It's totally okay to feel however you feel!* The more you accept and allow your feelings, the easier it is to move through them.

Feeling angry, anxious, irritated, sad, frustrated, or lonely is a totally normal, even expected part of the human condition. We experience these emotions from time to time, and some chapters of our lives make these feelings more prevalent than others. We lose family members, watch our children leave the nest, experience heartbreak and divorce, lose jobs, retire, and battle illness. While being aware of our lens on the world is critical to shaping our experience, it's also incredibly important to give ourselves permission to feel.

Sometimes our impulse is to turn away from those difficult feelings. After all, who wants to feel bad. We are afraid that if we submit to the feelings, they will sweep us away and leave us shipwrecked. Or worse, we'll do or say something we regret, so we stuff our emotions away in the bottom of the suitcase. When we turn toward our difficult emotions, they can flow through us instead of getting stuck. The experience of allowing feelings to flow through us becomes much more palatable if we remind ourselves that they are fleeting. When we stop resisting them, they flow like a river through us, often sweeping away the toxic debris, and we come out the other side cleansed and intact.

When we repeatedly shove the difficult emotions aside, we run the risk of those feelings taking a toxic toll on our bodies and minds. We begin to see those emotions manifest in other symptoms of dis-ease.[6] One surefire marker that we're not dealing with our sticky, gunky feelings is that they begin to come out sideways and unexpectedly. After all, there's only so much room in that suitcase!

It takes time to normalize this response to big feelings. As we learned in Chapters 1 and 2, many of us have developed a lens on the world that doesn't allow us to feel or manage our emotions in this way. Sometimes, our patterns and beliefs have been formed in a way that makes us feel uncomfortable or unsafe expressing ourselves. The brain is a miraculously pliable organ, and we can retrain it. As we start to carve new neural pathways, we make it easier to deal with our emotions in a healthy manner. Like riding a bike or learning to knit, we practice and give ourselves grace as we learn.

---

6   A state of imbalance that may result in emotions manifesting as physical symptoms.

Let's talk for a moment about what we mean by *giving yourself permission*. When you give yourself permission to be your whole self in a given moment, you're establishing a new pattern of behavior. This can look like loving yourself even at your messiest, while setting appropriate boundaries and trusting your alignment. Just like Sandi gave herself permission to feel wildly out of control and even scared while she began her city-dating adventure, and Stacie felt afraid of making mistakes in her relationship, we are all going to feel scared, angry, or out of alignment from time to time. That is the human condition! By giving ourselves permission to feel what we feel, we are taking the first step toward caring for ourselves and returning to our center.

PRACTICE GIVING YOURSELF PERMISSION

Let's identify three different ways you can explore the concept of giving yourself permission. These micro-moments can have an immense impact on your ability to give yourself permission and launch you on the road to authentic bliss. Just because they are small doesn't mean they won't begin to cause lasting shifts in your life.

The first of these ways is to engage your **curiosity**. In any given moment, whether it's a highly charged emotional situation or a simple joyous interaction, take a moment to notice what is happening inside. What is happening to your body? Do you feel a physical response to the situation—butterflies in your stomach, a flush in your cheeks, tears in your eyes? No need to do anything other than note it and label it.

Now that you've noticed your response to a situation and put some language to it, simply allow it to be. When you can name what is happening and why you are thinking or responding in a certain way, you'll experience a subtle shift of energy that accompanies a moment of calm and understanding. This second micro-moment is complex, simultaneously holding space for your emotions and labeling them without judgment. We call this ***giving yourself grace.*** There is no judgment in this moment, just a simple observation and acknowledgement of yourself.

The third micro-moment is when we invite ***acceptance.*** We allow ourselves to be exactly where we are without feeling the need to change, improve, or judge. We recognize that our journey is a dynamic one, filled with leaps forward, U-turns, switchbacks, and backtracks. This moment is just one moment in our journey, and that there are ample opportunities for shifts in the future. Allowing ourselves to be exactly where we are in a given moment gives us a powerful sense of agency. Then a wondrous thing happens; when we start noticing with curiosity, grace, and acceptance, our consciousness shifts.

As you try out these micro-moments, notice the sensations that come up. What clues is your body giving you as you check in with curiosity, grace, and acceptance? The more you try your hand at giving yourself permission, the more natural it will feel. As we intentionally engage in these practices, we are on our way to meaningful evolution: authentic, thoughtful change in our way of being in the world.

MEET OUR LITTLE SISTER, STEPHANIE

We'd like to introduce you to our youngest sister, Stephanie. She was born on Stacie's tenth birthday to our mom and stepdad. Stephanie is wicked smart and has been dealt enormous challenges along her journey. Some challenges we witnessed, and others occurred after we left for college. Stephanie has weathered it all, emerging with a sarcastic sense of humor and the ability to light up a room with her bountiful energy and infectious laughter. She's on a mission to make things happen, putting her four children and her husband at the top of her priority list. Stephanie can be real and raw in a way that encourages people to instantly feel comfortable sharing their struggles and concerns. She is always there for us, cheering on our wild ideas and celebrating with us along the way. We always know that she won't sugarcoat what we need to hear and yet her compassionate heart always leads the way.

We've included a couple of her authentically raw stories in celebration of our sisterhood, as well as an opportunity to share another example of how the journey of bliss evolves. Stephanie turned forty as we began writing this book. Her stories demonstrate where we were ten years ago, healing from trauma and navigating huge life transitions.

STEPHANIE: MY PATH TO PERMISSION

It was a weekend when I was supposed to be with Rocky, my father. I have trouble calling him my dad—honestly, he was never around. He was my biological father, but he wasn't really a dad. He and our mom separated when I was a baby. One weekend, I was going to stay with him, and for some reason the handoff was happening at the movie theater in Big Bear.

Mom dropped me off there in the early evening. I was sitting on my Barbie suitcase, which means I must have been about five or six. In retrospect, it seems insane that I was left alone at that age. Maybe one of my sisters was at the movies? I don't know. I just remember sitting on my suitcase, waiting and waiting. No one came.

Eventually, one of my mom's friends saw me sitting there and called her. She came to get me. Nothing bad happened, but it was one of my earliest memories of being left and forgotten. It taught me that if I didn't let anyone get close, then I wouldn't ever have to feel forgotten again.

I am the youngest sister. My view on the world is pretty cynical. For a long time, I believed that everyone was bad, and everything was dangerous. If you keep to yourself and stay in your bubble, you'll be safe. Keep everyone else out, build a wall around yourself, and then nothing can hurt you.

I learned over and over that no one else was going to keep me safe. No one else was going to show up on a consistent basis. No one else was going to be there always. It was just going to be me.

I operated like this for a long time. I had a wall up around me that no one could climb. When I was thirty-four, I drove my boyfriend across the state and was pulled over. Unbeknownst to me, he had drugs in the car. Before I knew it, I found myself in jail.

All sorts of things went through my mind as I sat there in the cell. I started thinking about all of these things I did wrong. I berated myself for making so many bad choices. I spiraled into thinking that I was a terrible person, that I deserved what had happened to me. The thing is: none of that thinking was helpful. I had to pull myself together and re-mind myself I wasn't a bad person. I had just made a dumbass mistake.

I wasn't in a place where I could love myself yet. That took many more steps. But I gave myself a little grace, and that was a turning point. I was released from jail and acquitted of all charges, but I still had lots of work to do.

It sounds weird to say, but I am grateful for being in jail. It was like getting hit with a Mack Truck. It forced me to wake the heck up and shift my thinking. I began to see that I was not defined by my past and that the future was still a blank page. That helped me shift my thinking from "I'm a bad person" to "I made some bad decisions."

When I met my husband, JJ, I was in a place where I could own my experience. I told him on our third date, "Look, this is what happened. This is my story. It's part of who I am." I was waiting for the shoe to drop, waiting for what he would say.

"Oh, my gosh. Were you okay? Are you okay now?" he asked. I was amazed. He was concerned about me, not what I'd done. There really were people that wouldn't judge me for my past.

There's a lot of work still to do. I still have lots of negative records playing in my head. When something challenging happens, those re-cords start playing again. It takes a lot of effort to interrupt them. The positive ones aren't written yet. Hopefully, one day they will be. I would definitely like to move faster toward that.

I still have a lot of walls up, but I'm allowing a few more people into the courtyard. My husband, my sisters, they get to come in. And having those people I trust give some positive feedback helps to pave the way.

PLAYGROUND OF PERMISSION

There are a couple of places to explore in the Playground of Permission: *self-compassion, self-love, self-respect,* and *self-trust*. When we first explored this idea, we thought of these as steps along a path. The more we've done our own exploration of these parts of giving ourselves permission, however, the more we've come to think of them as a playground.

When you were a kid and went to the park, you probably had a favorite piece of playground equipment. Maybe you preferred the swings, but if the swing set was full, you were game to play on the seesaw. We would like to invite you to approach these with a similar mindset. These concepts are all pieces of giving yourself permission, and we believe a healthy exploration of each is important, but depending on how you show up on any given day, you may be drawn more to one than another.

By having a variety of tools to draw upon, we're equipped to contend with whatever life throws our way. When we find ourselves in a moment of crisis or catapulted into unknown territory, we may not be at a place to navigate self-trust, so we return to compassion. What we need in any given moment will shift and change—this process is as dynamic as we are! The good news is that the more we practice, the easier it becomes to navigate. This allows us to move through our journey and not feel as dysregulated—the feeling of being out of emotional equilibrium—as we may have felt before.

SELF-COMPASSION

If giving yourself permission is new, it is important to start by learning to treat yourself with compassion. When we treat ourselves with care, we recognize that our reactions may be based upon what we've encountered throughout our lives. We have the ability to see that our experiences shape us, and rather than reacting with judgment or shame, we treat ourselves with loving kindness.

Dr. Krista Neff is a researcher at the University of Texas who studies self-compassion and is the cofounder of the Center for Mindful Self-Compassion. She articulates three elements of self-compassion:[7]

1. **Self-kindness vs. Self-judgment.** Being compassionate toward ourselves means extending warmth and understanding when we suffer, fail, or feel inadequate, rather than ignoring our pain or beating ourselves up.

2. **Recognizing Our Common Humanity vs. Isolation.** Recognizing that suffering and feelings of inadequacy are not just common but part of what makes us human allows us to see beyond ourselves. We are not alone!

3. **Mindfulness vs. Overidentification.** Mindfulness asks us to unflinchingly look directly at our pain rather than push it away. It suggests that by seeing our suffering with openness and clarity, we have an opportunity to treat ourselves with kindness in order to heal, while also not getting swept away by overidentifying with it.

When we treat ourselves with compassion, we talk to our inner selves the same way we would talk to our dearest friend.

Let's imagine for a moment that your best friend shows up at your front door in tears. She's had a meeting with her boss about her

7   Krista Neff, *Self-compassion: The Proven Power of Being Kind to Yourself* (HarperCollins, 2011).

performance. As her boss gave her critical feedback, your friend started to cry right there in her boss's office. Would you tell her she was unprofessional or inappropriate? Would you tell her she might as well polish off her resume and start looking for a new job? Of course you wouldn't. You'd envelop her with a giant hug. Then you'd remind her that she is a product of her environment and that perhaps she was triggered because her parents or coach expected her to perform perfectly and shamed her when she made a mistake. You'd love her deeply, empathize wholeheartedly, and help your dear friend see that what she sees as a catastrophic faux pas is likely a blip on the radar.

Learning to treat yourself with compassion is treating yourself the way you'd treat your best friend. You assume positive intentions, recall that you are not alone, recognize your behaviors and reactions, and love yourself through it.

SELF-LOVE

When we've learned to treat ourselves with compassion, we can begin to implement a daily practice of self-love. The key here is in the *practice*. The practice of self-love invites us to check in on ourselves every day. When we intentionally check in, we begin to notice which parts of ourselves could use a little care, and where we're feeling good. We begin to get to know ourselves deeply and recognize the peaks and valleys in our day-to-day existence.

Dr. Darcy Lord, author and self-love expert, reminds us that no matter what is going on in our day-to-day lives, whether we're at the top of a peak or in a valley, we have an opportunity to practice self-love.[8] She suggests that most of us are out of the habit of practicing self-love for a variety of personal and cultural reasons. Like riding a bicycle or getting in the habit of going to the gym, we have to start somewhere.

Now that we've gotten into the habit of noticing, we can take our

---

8   Dr. Darcy Lord, accessed April 24, 2022, https://drdarcylord.com.

observations a step further. When we observe ourselves feeling shame, embarrassment, or inferiority to others, rather than shake our finger at that part of ourselves, what if we offer it love? Dr. Lord suggests that first we say out loud: "This is evidence that I want to feel safe and loved. Of course, I want to feel safe and loved! Everyone wants to feel safe and loved!" Next, ask yourself what you need to do to be kind to yourself.

You might notice after putting in long hours at work finishing a project that you are more short-tempered than usual, and your neck is in knots. Aha! It's time to pause, recognize, and celebrate that you've accomplished a big goal! A long bath with some lavender Epsom salts might be in order. You've practiced self-love by noticing what you've accomplished and what you need in order to recharge.

SELF-RESPECT

Self-respect invites us to put our needs at the top of the list. Oftentimes people confuse permission and boundary setting. They are connected, but there is a distinction between the two. Giving yourself permission is the first step in the process of caring for yourself. Permission allows you to put your needs ahead of another person's wants. By giving yourself permission to be your full self, you're taking the first step toward creating boundaries.

As humans, we often feel as though we are being selfish by putting ourselves first. In order to navigate this, we've adopted a rule of thumb that helps to guide us in setting appropriate boundaries:

RULE OF THUMB: *Boundaries allow you to prioritize your own needs before someone else's wants. Acting selfishly is placing your wants over another person's needs.*

In 2010, at the airport with her children, Stacie had a glaring reminder of this lesson. Stacie was maintaining the delicate balance of keeping track of three kiddos while wrangling luggage when she saw an elderly woman struggling with her suitcase on the escalator. Stacie's impulse was to send her eldest daughter to help the elderly woman. Her ten-year-old daughter looked up at her and said, "Mom, we've got our hands full here, and you want me to go help someone else?"

The point was made: we have to make sure our immediate needs are addressed before we can be of service to anyone else. That's not selfish; that's just good sense. Stacie had to remind herself that she doesn't have to be the rescuer for everyone. Our children are so often our best teachers. Becoming comfortable with this is a huge challenge, especially for those who show love by being of service. The old cliché holds true: we must put our own oxygen masks on before we help anyone else with theirs.

When we set boundaries, we are drawing a line around ourselves and stating, "This gets to come in and that does not." We like to think of boundaries as rolling up the car window as we travel. We all have the agency to look out the window and assess the weather outside; if the weather is favorable, we can open the window wide. If it grows cold or rainy, perhaps we'll shut the window a bit, or even all the way. We have the ability to choose and adjust, depending on the situation. When we give ourselves permission to choose at any given moment, we are increasingly empowered. This empowerment is self-respect.

SELF-TRUST

Self-trust is when our heads, hearts, and guts are aligned, and we are secure in our place in the world.[9] Brené Brown has studied what she calls the anatomy of trust. She adopted the following definition of trust from Charles Feltman: "Trust is choosing to make something important to you vulnerable in the actions of someone else."

Armed with a definition, Brown went on to break the concept into its core components. Brown's acronym BRAVING is a wonderful guide

---

9   Brené Brown, *Rising Strong: How the Ability to Reset Transforms the Way We Live, Love, Parent, and Lead* (Random House, 2017).

to building trust in all sorts of situations. Each word is a critical component to establishing trust:

Boundaries: As we've discussed, creating clear boundaries for what is okay and not okay is the first step in developing a trusting relationship with yourself.

Reliability: You might be the most reliable person in your office, but do you show up for yourself? Do you recognize your limits and protect yourself from burnout?

Accountability: When you recognize that you haven't taken good care of yourself, do you acknowledge it and make amends? Do you find ways to shift that behavior?

Vault: You protect yourself. This doesn't mean you armor up for everyone, but you recognize that not everyone gets to be privy to your deepest vulnerabilities.

Integrity: You choose courage over comfort, as Brown says. You put your values into practice even when it is hard.

Nonjudgment: You can recognize what you need at any given time without judging yourself for it.

Generosity: You recognize the positive intentions, language, and action in yourself and celebrate it.

When we reach a place of self-trust, we can align what we know in our heads, our hearts, and our guts. Each of these systems has a job to do, and when we've got them working together, they are the ultimate safety net. Checking in with these systems becomes second nature, and we can glean information that will guide us in our next steps. We have practiced these steps forward and backward, and as a result, we are more secure in our place in the world and trust our intuition more often than not. We'll talk more in depth about self-trust and how it shows up in our journey in the next chapter.

GIVING OTHERS PERMISSION

When we begin to give ourselves permission to love ourselves, give ourselves grace, treat ourselves with compassion, and put our needs before others' wants, we are not just taking radically good care of ourselves. We are also modeling this behavior for others. Even when we are perfectly imperfect, we are showing those around us that it's okay to learn and grow. The impact of allowing ourselves permission to BE is our beautiful gift to the world.

Our children will often teach us the most important lessons of all. Before they started dating, Stacie often ran into Roland at the library where he worked as a librarian and where her daughter, Amelia, was enrolled in a tutoring program. One day when she arrived to pick Amelia up from tutoring, she and Roland struck up a conversation, as they often did, and he invited her to coffee. Amelia climbed up on the chair beside them and spoke very clearly and directly to Roland.

"She doesn't like coffee. She doesn't like beer. And she doesn't like buffets."

While they chuckled at her precociousness, Stacie was also struck that Amelia understood very clearly what it meant to set clear boundaries and expectations. At the tender age of nine, she was learning the importance of recognizing the ways to honor our needs and intentionally communicate them. As a parent, Stacie was flooded with pride and gratitude for this smart, brave little girl, and simultaneously realized that dating with children required discretion and more navigation than it did when she was in her twenties.

Through our own behavior, we are teaching our children, families, friends, and colleagues how to engage with us and what is acceptable in our presence. When we begin on the path to permission and learn to care for ourselves, giving ourselves the permission to feel and set boundaries, then we are setting an example for all those around us.

KEY NUGGETS:

- ✎ Giving ourselves permission to be where we are at any given moment is critical to our healing.

- ✎ Loving our messy selves allows us to be who we are fully.

- ✎ When we allow ourselves to play in the Playground of Permission, we build our skills in self-compassion, self-love, and self-respect.

- ✎ Giving ourselves permission is the first step toward setting compassionate, loving boundaries.

- ✎ When we embody these things, we begin to show others the importance of permission as well.

Chapter 5
ALIGNING YOUR
INTERNAL COMPASS

We talked about self-trust a bit in Chapter 4. We unpacked Brené Brown's BRAVING acronym and explored the ways to reach self-trust. If you recall, *self-trust is when our heads, hearts, and guts are aligned, and we are secure in our place in the world.* In this chapter, we'd like to dig deeper into how to continue cultivating that trust in yourself so you can begin to identify your core values. This will free you to tap into your personal superpower. Self-trust is the innate compass that helps guide us on our way.

Just like the path to permission, developing self-trust isn't a one-and-done situation. Self-trust is a practice that we hone over time, that we constantly readdress as we evolve. Like all skill development, it requires intentional practice, patience, and sometimes coaching.

Self-trust requires us to recognize when we are out of alignment with our circumstances but perhaps even more importantly, when we have violated our own values. Many of us work hard to nurture and care for the people in our lives—children, partners, clients, students, coworkers—at the expense of our own needs. Being aware of when we've let ourselves down is a critical component of unpacking our bliss.

CYCLE OF PACKING AND UNPACKING

We've learned that there is not a direct route through this healing journey because there is no endpoint. It is a cycle of packing and unpacking. Both the beauty and the challenge of our existence is the fact that we are ever-evolving. Our existence is dynamic. Learning to trust our inner knowing is an important step on the road to bliss.

The most obvious way to observe self-trust is to get curious about our decision-making. The way we make decisions gives us feedback on whether or not we are aligned and reminds us of how to anchor into self-trust. If we make a decision and feel out of sorts about the outcome, we may have made it from a place that is out of alignment with who we truly are and what we want. That's okay! This is information that allows us to learn and grow. If we realize that we're heading in a direction that isn't aligned with our essence, we recalibrate.

Ideally, we make our decisions when our nervous systems are calm and when we feel centered. Sometimes, however, we're in a situation that causes us to be out of alignment, and we're faced with making a decision. In these situations, we invite you to return to these simple questions: *Am I safe? What do I need to do to make myself safe?*

This allows us to respond in alignment with our values, though that doesn't always happen. Making decisions based on fear, anger, or resentment may intentionally or unintentionally harm others. These decisions are choices that take us in a new direction. We're going to dig into discovering our core values in Chapter 6.

Ultimately, the "destination" on our journey is building a new skill or developing a new way of thinking. The more we evolve our consciousness, the more adept we become at aligning to our values and making those course corrections when necessary.

Before we had Google Maps to tell us how to get from point A to point B, before we had a road atlas to refer to, humans developed ways to orient themselves. We used the stars, our shadows, and landmarks to point us in the direction we hoped to go. The skills we've developed in the first chapters of the book have become part of your tote bag of skills to navigate forward.

By now, you have:

- ✍ Learned to think about your thinking

- ✍ Begun to identify the stories that don't serve you

- ✍ Started to shift into thinking on purpose

- ✍ Embarked upon a path of giving yourself permission, thereby allowing you to trust yourself

You have the tools to help you identify the clues that are arising in your soul. While there may not be a roadmap, there is a process.

Self-Awareness → Self-Regulation → Self-Advocacy

We start by getting to know ourselves; then we are able to witness our feelings and sensations, which gives us valuable information. Then we ask questions: *Is our initial impression of ourselves true? Can we find ways to refute our assumptions about ourselves? Can we shift our thinking and lean into our strengths?*

We were all forced to learn new ways of doing things over and over again during the COVID-19 pandemic. Even the simplest things like going to the grocery store or interacting with our neighbors suddenly required more forethought than ever before. On top of that, we're all navigating new things all the time, so the layers of newness were piling up!

Stacie remembers having a discussion with her oldest daughter, Sabina, about navigating this new reality.

"Everything requires so much thought. It's all so new," Stacie said exasperatedly.

"What do you mean? Parenting isn't new!" Sabina exclaimed.

"Of course it is! I've been parenting for years, but I've never parented young adults. That's all new too."

Stacie's knee-jerk reaction was to think that she wasn't good at navigating new things. When she leaned in and interrogated that thought pattern, though, she was able to shift that thinking. *That is not the whole story,* she thought. *I may not look like I'm in my flow when trying new things, but I am good at observing. I'm good at asking for instructions, and I'm comfortable making mistakes. I can use my strengths to navigate what is uncomfortable.*

Stacie was able to notice that her thought patterns weren't serving her and began to self-regulate by challenging and shifting those thought patterns. She then defined the aligned actions she was committed to taking moving forward.

THE MOST IMPORTANT RELATIONSHIP IS WITH YOURSELF

All relationships require us to learn about one another, thereby establishing a mutual sense of trust. When we think of relationships, we think of them like a joint bank account. You and your partner each put resources into the relationship account. From time to time, one of you needs to make a big withdrawal; for example, one half of the relationship has lost a loved one and needs extra support or wants to make a major job change that takes a leap of faith. Because you've both been cultivating the relationship bank account, there are enough resources available to draw upon to bolster your partnership.

In this case, you are building a relationship with yourself. You've been learning about what made you who you are, how your patterns and behaviors show up in your life, and how to treat yourself with compassion. You've cultivated a beautiful relationship with yourself, and now you have resources in your relationship bank. We refer to this relationship as **self-awareness**. Self-awareness comes from practicing those three guideposts we keep referring to: *noticing, curious inquiry,* and *aligned action.* It allows us the ability to stop and evaluate what's going on in our bodies and minds and the situation around us. Stacie was able to notice the discomfort and dis-ease in her body and connect it to what she was experiencing in the moment. She was then able to explore self-critical thinking with grace and reframe her experience.

Once you've built this self-awareness, you begin to **self-regulate**. Self-regulation simply means monitoring and managing our own thoughts (self-talk), inner processes, emotions, and behaviors. We are able to wonder about what our body's clues are telling us through self-awareness. Perhaps you're having a discussion with your partner when you suddenly feel flushed and your heart begins racing. What is this bodily clue telling you? What triggered this response? Perhaps your partner used a phrase that brings up a belief from your childhood, which in turn activates a response. Our self-awareness causes us to stop and evaluate. Our self-regulatory skills help us address whether the response is aligned before proceeding.

Self-regulation comes from knowing ourselves, recognizing where our beliefs and stories come from, and choosing to recalibrate to the lens we want to use. We return to being settled and centered so we can take the most appropriate action. Stacie was able to recognize that her response was not entirely aligned with the person she knows herself to be. She was able to recall the skills and strengths that she can draw upon: to observe, ask for directions, and be comfortable making mistakes. She realigned and was able to move forward from a place of centeredness.

When we've gotten curious about our response in the moment, determined its root, and taken a moment to recalibrate to our most aligned selves, we can **self-advocate** for what we need. Perhaps in the moment, we ask our partner to rephrase their statement, or we even take a breather from the conversation. Self-advocacy is our ability to know what we need *and* then work to have those needs met. Closely related to agency and empowerment, self-advocacy is the beautiful outcome of knowing ourselves, being centered in that knowing, and then taking action to create the circumstances we want and need. When we are self-aware and regulated, we can make decisions and take actions that best serve our highest good. When the practice of self-regulation happens in micro-moments, the big moments are easier to manage.

Remember that relationship bank? Return to this concept of being in a relationship with yourself. When you are continually making withdrawals from the bank account you have for yourself, you will eventually run dry. When you are in a trusting, honest relationship with yourself, you'll know when you've overdrawn the bank account and then take steps to rectify the situation.

We know we've really cultivated trust in ourselves when the proverbial shit hits the fan. When things are flowing and life is feeling easy, trust in ourselves likely feels more or less natural. But when life throws us curve balls, we discover just how much our faith in our inner knowing pays off.

We will all encounter setbacks, tragedy, and challenge. There is no enlightened space that insulates us from the inevitabilities of life. But when we are truly grounded in ourselves, when our self-knowledge and belief in ourselves is strong, we are able to find our way through the most difficult of circumstances. Our self-trust is our compass guiding us through the thick fog.

SANDI: BUILDING A NEW NEST

I arrived at Logan Airport at 5:30 a.m. on December 30, 2022, and everything fell into place just as I planned. Even things I expected to go sideways went like clockwork, except for the parts I could have never imagined nor planned for—the feelings that unfolded after the moving-in chaos subsided.

My sisters and their hubbies showed up in perfect timing, thirty minutes after the movers had finished unloading the truck into my new home. What happened for the next four days was so humbling and inspiring that I can only say it was guided by a universal love greater than I can describe.

My kitchen was unpacked in less than three hours with sticky notes on all the cabinets for us to remember where we decided to put things. My brothers-in-law made more trips to the hardware store than were actually needed, but who was I to stop their brotherly bonding adventures? I asked them to rearrange the living room furniture just enough times to not drive everyone crazy, and they hung my TV in the perfect location with the wires all tucked nicely, just like a professional crew. My sisters organized my closets in a fraction of the time it would have taken me—it helps to have an extra set of hands and sister telepathy on your side. The things I would have had to hire a handyman for were fixed before I even knew they were broken. And we were all able to connect over wonderful meals each night, with a special New Year's Eve celebration topped off with a super yummy family-cooked lobster dinner because, when in New England, you must kick off the adventure with lobster!

With my home "put together" and filled with the love of my family, it was time for them to head back to Florida and Texas. I spent the next few days busying myself with more home-nesting details and work meetings. I was so happy with my new beginning!

And yet, I found that I didn't want to work or set up my office. I didn't want to dive into tasks and meetings and projects that felt like the same old routine in a different location. All I wanted was to sit in a coffee shop and write and feel into what I needed each day without any preconceived "shoulds." I had been forcing myself to "accomplish the things" and check the boxes of getting settled into a new home, a new town, a new rhythm, a whole new world. I felt like I had to keep driving my businesses forward and keep sharing with everyone that "everything is great, and I am safe and happy." I suffocated myself with obligations and "shoulds." As the days went by, I found myself trying to push through and stuff down the feelings.

Thankfully, after years of practicing unpacking my bliss, I am learning to speak up for what I truly need, recognizing and articulating when I feel selfish for doing so. This time it took me a couple of weeks to get there, which felt much better than a couple of decades.

I knew what I needed: my sister.

We had a Zoom meeting scheduled to map out the keynote for a conference where we were going to speak. Instead of joining Zoom, I picked up the phone and called.

"I can't breathe, and I don't want to let you down," I said.

"How can I support you? And by the way, you're not letting me down. I'm here for you, and we're in this together," she replied.

Stacie leaned in with her sisterly love, and so, with that safe space and permission to feel, I was able to unwind. I was exhausted by the micro decisions I had to make each day. I was overwhelmed and happy at the same time.

"I don't want to share this with anyone and have them say, 'Well, you didn't have to move,'" I told Stacie. "Because for my soul's purpose, I needed to do this. And it's still freaking hard!"

I needed to go back to the beginning of my practice, give myself permission to feel what I feel and to get curious about where these limiting beliefs were coming from. I believed I needed to have everything figured out in five minutes and settled and perfect. I was trapped in a binary thinking pattern: If I was happy with my decision, then I couldn't also be overwhelmed. I gave myself permission to ask for what I needed, even if it felt like I was asking for too much. My sister helped me remember that we can all feel multiple things at the same time—that's the beauty of our human experience. After listening to Stacie's soothing voice, I remembered that I get to ask for what I need and share what I am feeling.

Like Bambi learning to walk on his wobbly legs, I am designing, creating, and living through every micro decision. Doing this is more challenging than I dreamed it to be. All of the moving around gave me the gift of knowing the logistics of settling into a new home. Now I'm learning how to embrace all the emotions and feelings that go along with moving, let alone moving across the country, and being grounded in my home. I'm practicing receiving support from family and friends, old and new. I'm learning to be truly connected with this human experience of living an authentically blissful life!

I am grateful for this work, the tools and strategies, and the incredible humans I have surrounding me and supporting me. Rewiring and strengthening the neural pathways of self-trust takes consistent practice and awareness. It's definitely not always easy, yet it's always worth it sitting on the other side. This becomes crystal clear as I feel the bliss from finally sitting in a coffee shop in a small New England town, writing my book—just as I dreamed of doing when I knew I needed to move across the country and begin again.

The journey is never a straight line. The process of coming into my own self-awareness allowed me to begin to self-regulate my own nervous system and eventually advocate for my needs. Those cycles, just like all travelers' journeys, required me to travel inward so that I could move outward.

While self-trust allows you to relax into the best, most instinctive version of yourself, there's more to this adventure than self-knowledge. When you are truly able to trust yourself, you are laying the foundation for the beautiful, expansive work of digging into your core values and opening into your superpower. This is where the traveler's journey inward begins to simultaneously move outward, and our self-development begins to impact the world.

STACIE: TRUSTING MY FEELINGS

On February 14, 2018, a gunman entered a school located less than three hours from where I live and where, as a school psychologist, I provide therapeutic support to children in and outside of the school setting. Because we are hyper-connected to local and world events almost instantaneously through the news and social media, it was as if I was watching this tragedy unfold in real time as I wrapped up my day at one of the elementary schools I serve.

The next morning, I made a plan with the school counselor to begin my day at the elementary school on campus, and she would support students at the upper campus across the street. As I drove toward
the school in North Port, I felt a strong pull to just keep driving toward Parkland, Florida, and to be present and provide support for the
Marjorie Stoneman Douglas students and parents who had suffered
devastating losses the previous day. I am a helper by nature, and that
part of me felt the compulsion to be of service, but I also knew that my
students would need me that day.

I entered the school building, not considering the possibility that
the elementary school children in North Port might have been exposed
to their older siblings' social media posts about the chaos of the previous day. I'd briefly forgotten that elementary-age children have limited
sense of time and space (the whole state of Florida felt like a very close-
knit community at that time); I was wrapping my head around the idea
that if a child felt unsafe at home, now they had direct evidence to feel
unsafe at school. I was determined and prepared to support the adults
in the building. I wasn't entirely prepared for the depth of fear that was
physically observable in some of our elementary-age students. To hold
space for both students and faculty meant I had to put my own unease
and fear aside.

I spent a majority of my morning with three elementary students
who had previously experienced family trauma and were in a state of
extreme panic because they now felt unsafe at school. Due to my own
upbringing and sense of purpose, I have always felt a deep need to keep
children psychologically and physically safe. The world that day felt
very unsafe, and my job increasingly heavy.

I held my sadness in all day. Later, I showed up late to a meeting
that Sandi was holding via Zoom with the educators at the school in
North Port, Florida. I walked in the door, and although I deeply wanted to continue holding space for others, when a fellow educator enveloped me in a hug, the tears began to fall.

"I just want to keep them safe," I said. One of my fundamental core values is the desire to keep children safe, and this day challenged me in ways I hadn't expected. I didn't want to let my emotions burst out of me, but I was so overwhelmed. Letting myself break down was unsettling, but it also felt good to cry. I was experiencing so much sadness and mounting grief, recognizing the loss for parents and family, as well as the students' loss of close friends and the teachers' loss of students— their feelings of failing, as part of a network of nurturers and healers within this society, to keep our most treasured commodity safe.

Retelling this story reminded me that emotions don't need to be let out in a controlled fashion in a demonstration of emotional intelligence. Rather, experiencing and sharing genuine feelings can create a stronger bond between colleagues and friends. In fact, when you wrangle your emotions too tightly and only release them in a controlled way, you risk having a performative emotional response, and that doesn't build trust in the same way. When you allow yourself to respond authentically, those around you are given permission to do the same.

KEY NUGGETS

- When we develop an honest, intimate relationship with ourselves, we deepen self-awareness, which leads us to the ability to self-regulate or manage our systems. When we can do that, we can self-advocate for our needs from a centered, grounded place.

- Self-trust allows us to listen to our own inner knowing to guide us through the most difficult, foggy chapters.

- It is a journey, and we are always learning more and honing our ability to listen to ourselves.

Chapter 6

THE VALUES THAT DRIVE YOU

FINDING AND ORIENTING YOUR COMPASS

In the last five chapters, you've learned how to better understand yourself, where your beliefs and behaviors stem from, and taken the first steps to self-awareness. All these tools are essential for the next step on your journey to authentic bliss: to identify and work with your core values. By uncovering and articulating these values, you will be able to live according to what resonates with you.

Core values are the characteristics and traits that make us tick. They are the compass that helps guide us on our journey. These characteristics are the principles and ethics that drive our decision-making and most importantly, help us assess our sense of alignment. Core values are our guidebook for life and how we behave.

Oftentimes, people use the phrase "core values" interchangeably with the word "beliefs." We discussed the ways beliefs are formed in Chapter 1: through learned behavior and unconscious patterning, we develop beliefs about how the world works. This can unfold in lots of ways. We learn from what we are taught, view, or experience. Beliefs are something we are convinced are true, even without having evidence. In other words, they aren't empirical truths or absolute truths.

They often affect the way we *see* the world.

A value, however, is a principle or ideal that we live by, and it reflects what we believe is important. Our values affect how we *behave* in the world. This is a subtle but critical distinction. Beliefs can shift and change. Values, while they often evolve, are deeply embedded in who we are.

What's the difference between a value and a *core value*? A value is something we collectively recognize is worthy and important. We all hold many common societal or socially acceptable values; our *core* values, however, are viscerally, deeply important to each of us as individuals. One person's core values may differ greatly from another's. Core values are a value on steroids.

Oftentimes the term *core value* brings to mind the poster on the wall of your office listing the thing that your employer values. Maybe you learned about them during your employee onboarding, maybe they come up at the annual meeting, but otherwise you don't give them much thought. Those core values are likely not working as they were intended.

Tony Hsieh, Sandi's dear friend and the late CEO of Zappos, framed core values differently and articulates this in his book *Delivering Happiness*.[10] To his mind, the core values of a company are reflected in everything they do: how they interact with customers, vendors, and each other. They are the values that are the framework for all decisions, *and* they define who you are as a group. Those core values are reflected and defined by the culture you work in and live by. In fact, he even said that the core values are so endemic to the workforce of Zappos that employees live by them both on and off the job.

Similarly, we have core values as family units—and this is a distinction from our beliefs. The core values of one Midwestern family of five will be different from those of the Midwestern family of five living around the corner.

Have you ever focused on your personal core values? We think

---

10   Tony Hsieh, *Delivering Happiness: A Path to Profits, Passion, and Purpose* (Grand Central Publishing, 2013).

of them as our special, unique imprint, like a fingerprint. These core values are responsible for driving the bus of our life, and we each have a distinctive set. If we don't know what they are, then we are blindly sitting in the back of the bus, holding on for dear life. When we are grounded in the knowledge of our imprint, then we can work in partnership with our core values to live intentionally, firmly anchored in our power. We are driving the bus.

Let's look at an example: Most of us would agree that honesty is a valuable trait. We do our best to tell the truth, and we appreciate when others are honest with us. If our partner fibs about sneaking the last cookie from the cookie jar, we might be annoyed, but we won't lose any sleep over the transgression.

For someone with a *core* value of honesty, truth is nonnegotiable. They feel the violation of this value at the gut level. Therefore, a lie about the cookie would shake them to their core. It may show up in their body as an elevated heart rate or a clenched jaw. Everything in them feels out of place. For them, dishonesty is a dealbreaker.

When our values are out of alignment, it can be as simple as the feeling of having a pebble in our shoe or a clothing tag scratching our skin, and as extreme as the feeling that everything in our world is working against us. We may feel a sense of unease or discomfort, or as if everything is all out of whack. When we are living in alignment with our core values, everything flows.

SANDI: MY CORE VALUE OF GRATITUDE

When Hunter was three years old, I was on the brink of losing my mind. I was a mom at my wit's end with a kid who was acting like many toddlers do: demanding, ungrateful, and selfish. Any parent of a toddler will appreciate the monumental amount of patience they require, and my child was no different. One day, though, this lack of appreciation pushed all my buttons. I found myself wildly debating taking the kid's bedroom door off its hinges and stuffing all his toys in a garbage bag. My internal monologue raged: *This kid has it so good! Why is he acting this way?*

Then, I stopped. *This is not the parent I want to be,* I thought. On a bit of a whim, I turned to Hunter and asked him to tell me three things he was grateful for. It took a couple of times of me asking; then something in him shifted, and the energy between us shifted too. I knew I was onto something important.

From then on, I made it a habit to help Hunter take a pause to check in with gratitude. As he grew older, he began to do the same for me. At the time, I didn't realize this as one of my core values. When I began doing the work to identify my personal core values, I could see how gratitude was a foundational value for me.

UNCOVERING YOUR CORE VALUES

Let's walk through some exercises that may help you reveal the guiding principles that make up your personal set of core values. Grab your journal and your favorite pen. Spend some time with any or all of these activities and circle back to them as often as needed. There are no right or wrong answers—just write from the heart.

Activity 1: Whisper Brand

We learned this activity through the Renegade Global accelerator program with our mentor and friend, AmyJo Martin, and realized how powerful it is to gain an honest perspective from those with whom we surround ourselves on the impression we give others.

Send an email to five individuals with various degrees of connection to you that reads something like: "I am working on understanding my 'whisper brand,' which is what people think of when they think about me. I'm asking people from different aspects of my life for input, honest feedback about the impression I make on individuals professionally and personally. Would you mind sharing the top three or four words that come to mind when you think of me?"

When Stacie did this activity, the five individuals she queried were enthusiastic about their responses and quickly replied. Their responses were reflective of how Stacie wants to show up in the world and led her to ponder whether these "values words" are core values or simply values she agrees with:

Attentive

Intentional

Considerate

Trustworthy

Subject Matter Expert

Focused

Proactive

Caring

Passionate

Entrepreneur

Visionary

Generous

Open-minded

Determined

Kind and Loving

Conscientious of Others

Activity 2: Toast to Yourself

This activity is from a training designed for educators that includes an exercise to practice positive self-talk.[11] It allows us to really think through what we want to be remembered for, how we want to show up in the world, and what is at the heart of it all.

---

11   Wayfinder, 2024, https://www.withwayfinder.com/.

Complete the following sentences:
One thing I like about myself . . .
One thing that makes me *me* . . .
One thing I'm proud of . . .
One thing I'm good at . . .

Upon completing the sentences above, craft the phrases into "A Toast to Yourself" with the identity of the person revealed at the end with the phrase, "And that person is me." The exercise provides a snapshot of what you value in yourself, your abilities, and your achievements. Unless you regularly journal, this exercise asking how you feel about yourself may feel awkward. It takes practice to notice what we are doing well and what we value in ourselves. Trust that it will reveal a perspective into your authentic core values.

Activity 3: Defining your Core Values

Defining your core values takes time and thoughtfulness to articulate what truly guides your unique fingerprint. The following questions allow you to get curious with your behaviors on a daily basis and reveal the core values that allow you to live in alignment with your truest self.

Answer these questions from your first instinct. There is no need to be elaborate in your answers; simply jot down what comes to mind.

- You have a whole day alone with no pressing obligations. What would you choose to do?
- What's really important to you?
- What always upsets you?
- What drives your decision-making on a daily basis?
- What is your indicator for a successful decision?
- What do you absolutely have to have in place to feel at ease?
- What characteristics are at play when you feel you are happiest or most inspired?

Do you notice particular values coming up over and over? Are certain values linked to big emotions? These are clues that lead you to your personal set of core values.

One of the best ways to uncover your core values is to ask yourself where you feel big emotions. Notice where you documented strong feelings, and then examine what those feelings are associated with. If the feeling is one of dis-ease, it points to a violation of a core value. When Hunter was behaving like an ungrateful child, Sandi got angry. She felt her pulse thudding in her ears; she wanted to scream and cry. His lack of appreciation pointed to what was truly important to her: gratitude.

Consider the times when you feel most out of balance. What makes you angry or sad? Where do you feel it in your body? Why does it elicit this response? What is the opposite of that? What core value has been breached? It may not have been crossed by another person; in fact, you may notice this feeling of being out of balance when you have infringed upon your own values.

Remember to be kind to yourself as you unpack your core values. Utilizing the three guideposts of noticing, getting curious, and then taking aligned action will help as you navigate through this discovery process.

When we do the work to unpack our set of core values, we can begin to use them in a variety of ways. When your values are aligned in your world, you feel good. Things seem to flow more easily. Your system is regulated, and you feel at ease. It's easier to notice the good in yourself and others. Learning new skills and having conscious conversations feels less troublesome.

Sandi: My Core Values as an Example

After dedicating a year to the thoughtful development of these core values, I make it a yearly practice to revisit and realign with them. I offer them here as both a guide and an example, encouraging you to articulate and draft your own unique core values as you live your life on purpose.

ॐ Love/Trust/Compassion/Empathy

Love means unconditional compassion and empathy, trusting in each other through thick and thin, the freedom to show up authentically in all areas of life. I know I have love in my life when I feel safe to be all me in any circumstance, when I feel seen and supported, and when I'm able to give the same to others.

ॐ Gratitude

Gratitude means savoring what is, appreciating the world and the people around me. It means having perspective and showing generosity of thoughts, words, and actions to those around me. I know gratitude is present in my life when I feel centered and grounded in all I am blessed with, down to the simplest of details and experiences.

ॐ Health

Health means taking care of my overall wellbeing, mentally, spiritually, physically, emotionally, and intellectually. It means eating what fuels my body, mind, and soul. It means exercising in ways that bring me joy and give me a strong, toned body. It means growing and learning consistently to feed my mind in ways that ignite and satisfy my curiosity. It means feeling all of my emotions with loving grace. I know I am healthy when I feel vibrant, authentic, and safe.

ॐ Wealth/Freedom

Wealth means the freedom to live and experience in vivid color! It means the ability to play and work in flow with my joy. It means being surrounded by amazing people who are aligned with my values and living from an abundance mindset. I know I am wealthy when I feel the success of money, experiences, and relationships around me with magnetic attraction and limitless flow. I feel financially wealthy when I have a steady stream of revenue flowing easily and effortlessly to me and through my businesses, allowing me to live in a home I love, travel, and experience the richness of life surrounded by beautiful people and things.

ᔌ Joy/Excitement

Joy means the excitement of life! Joy is an unending well of happiness and bliss to draw from. Joy means feeling uplifted, powerful, and magnetic. Joy is also peaceful abundance and being grateful for the alignment of all of my values at play. I know I have joy when I'm excited to get out of bed each day and find myself dancing randomly during the day.

ᔌ Play/Adventure

Play is a childlike sense of wonder and adventure. Play means freedom to explore, create, and wander, to experience all that life has to offer. Play means freedom to let loose of all fears of what anyone else thinks and to just go with the flow of adventure and joy. I know I have play in my life when I smile and laugh often as I get to experience all kinds of adventures with people I love.

ᔌ Serenity/Spirituality

Serenity leads to connecting with my spirituality, and my spirituality leads me to serenity and peace. Meditation and flow lead to hearing my authentic intuitive heart. I know I am living in alignment with serenity when I feel a certainty in my heart no matter the outcome, when I trust in the process of life and am detached from the outcome . . . enjoying the flow of serendipity.

ᔓ **Connection/Community**

Connection means creating a sense of belonging with those around me and attracting a values-aligned tribe of family and friends—my community to experience life with— knowing we all are loved and supported for the unique amazing humans we all are. I know I have this when I feel fulfilled each day, savoring my connections that are authentic and filled with love and grace.

ᔓ **Making a Difference/Passion/Purpose**

Making a difference in this life means living aligned with my greater purpose and feeling passionate about my work and my contribution to this world. I know I'm living this life when I "can't not do this work" and wake up most days excited to connect with my community and to create new ways to inspire them.

ᔓ **Vivid Lens**

Vivid lens means paying attention to environment and experience-enriching details for myself and those around me. It means savoring the details of this life and soaking it all in. I know I have it when I feel the vibrance of life in each experience no matter the context. This is the essence of living in alignment with my values each day!

ᔏ

Effective Communication

Once you are aware of and working with your core values, you have a whole new treasure chest of information and language to use at your disposal. You recognize how you behave when your values are out of whack, and you are empowered to communicate that to your partners, children, colleagues, and community. Perhaps more importantly, because you are aware of your values and recognize when they've been crossed, you can respond in a more clear, constructive way.

Purposeful Decision-Making

Decisions aren't good or bad. Despite what we've been programmed to believe, decision-making isn't binary. There are decisions that are made in alignment with your values, and they are the "right" decisions for you. Those choices may not be the best ones for someone else. After all, their circumstances and values may be different. When we are aligned with our core values, we can make decisions despite the outside chatter. Whatever may be the outcome of a decision, you know your choice is one that feels resonant and is in line with your values.

Being Seen, Heard, and Valued

By sharing your core values, you allow people to know you. They understand you in a way that allows you to be seen. Ultimately, being seen, heard, and valued is what we all seek at our core. It is the basis for healthy relationships and interdependence in this life.

SANDI: UNPACKING CORE VALUES VS. CORE WOUNDS

My core value of gratitude is rooted in my perception of not having enough as a child. We weren't always able to have the things we needed, much less wanted. Our Cabbage Patch dolls were homemade because we couldn't afford the store-bought versions (and our Nana made excellent substitutes, complete with their own birth certificates and tags that said *Made with Love from Nana*). Even when I was at a point where I could provide my son with whatever he needed, his perceived lack of gratitude triggered me.

Not every core value comes from a core wound, and not every core wound develops into a core value. While my experience was challenging, and it instilled a deep sense of gratitude in me, it didn't result in a core wound. I believe that is because I had the opportunity to see gratitude play out in a multitude of ways. Gratitude was modeled for us as focusing on connection, treasuring what we had because it came from the heart.

Our Nana grew up as one of twelve children in Hays, Kansas, before moving to Southern California. She didn't have much. But when we visited her in Norwalk, California, it didn't matter that there was only one bathroom and no spare bedroom. All the cousins piled in and rolled out sleeping bags on the floor. We were together; it was joyful and fun. We were loved deeply, and we knew that we had a multitude of blessings in this nurturing place. In addition, our paternal grandmother, Mama Lupe, was raised in a rural town in Mexico, and her home in California was filled with love. Each grandchild and almost every great-grandchild stayed with her and delighted in the nurturing environment. We often gathered around the banquette in her kitchen waiting for enchiladas, the smallest of us propped up on the booster seat.

So while there were challenges and hardships, there was also balance and connection, which fostered and expanded my core value of gratitude. And this core value continues to be a driving force for me every day.

While our adverse childhood experiences could have instead fostered a core wound around lack of gratitude, that's not the way it happened. Core wounds often appear when there is a pattern of experience, and the intensity is overwhelming. So if there is a pattern of scarce resources in your family, and that pattern results in overwhelming concern for your safety and security, the situation is ripe for a core wound to develop.

But let's say you have a caregiver who helps create as much normalcy as possible during this extremely stressful time. They hold space for your feelings, give you a chance to unpack the experience, and do their best to keep you safe. So the situation, which potentially could have become a core wound, instead simply becomes a piece of your story.

STACIE: UNPACKING MY CORE VALUE OF TOGETHERNESS

The wounds that we heal and develop into core values are special. My core value of togetherness and inclusivity stems from a core wound. As a child, I was witness to our parents' contentious divorces. The dissolution of our family unit was heartbreaking. I also spent a significant portion of my youth feeling like an outsider looking in. I have a strong desire to feel a sense of belonging. As an adult, I am determined to do everything in my power to create a cohesive, connected family. And yet, it took some time for me to recognize that this craving for togetherness might have a core wound at its root. Through a lot of processing and reflection, however, I was able to integrate that wound into my story, and it became a beautiful core value that motivates me.

Before I did the work to process my core wound, my reactions to a lack of togetherness were different. In the years between 2000 and 2002, when my family lived near Sandi's in Vegas, I had a vision of family dinners on Sundays. What I didn't realize was that Sandi's mother-in-law already planned Sunday dinners for her family, meaning that Sandi, her husband, and her son already had plans. I was deeply disappointed, but I didn't have the skills or ability to articulate my feelings at the time. So instead, I just shrugged them off, and when my family and I moved away, I thought, *It's alright. It wasn't the way I'd hoped it would be anyway.* Despite our closeness at the time, direct, heartfelt conversations were a challenge as Sandi and I both avoided communicating in a way that might make the other feel uncomfortable or burdened.

Lots of core values come from core wounds. When we have processed the core wound, we are no longer reacting in unproductive, passive-aggressive, or reactive ways. When we are able to respond in loving, generous ways, we have transitioned the core wound into a core value.

The key is in articulating the experience. When you can identify what is upsetting, then you can lean into what feels prickly and
hair-raising and reflect on why you're beginning to process that wound.
Therapy, of course, is an excellent way to do this. As we continue to
know ourselves even more deeply, we are able to unpack challenging
experiences in real time. *Why am I reacting this way? What am I noticing in my body? What is this bringing up for me? What is the lesson I can
take away from this?*

My children know that togetherness is deeply important to me.
Because I have been able to integrate what was once a core wound and
transition it to a core value, I am able to communicate my needs and
desires in a healthy, connected way.

In December 2021, I planned a family trip to Italy to assist my
youngest in getting settled for her semester abroad. I am a huge advocate for study abroad experiences, and I was thrilled about bringing all
of my grown children together. My stepson, however, procrastinated
about renewing his passport and ultimately wasn't able to join us on
the trip. If I hadn't worked with my core wound and unpacked the baggage that came with it, I could easily have been deeply hurt by this and
created tension in our relationship. Instead, I chose to have a frank conversation with my stepson. The conversation shifted when I was able
to articulate why this was important to me, and he was able to share
that he couldn't quite get the details together to make the trip happen.
What could have been interpreted as my stepson having an aversion to
being with the family became a more supportive conversation.

⚘

In our experience, even after all of this unpacking, violations of our
core values can still trigger the heck out of us; we are only human, after
all. We have had a conversation or two in which we unpack trigger
points like these. But when we are cognizant of our values, behaviors,
beliefs, and lens on the world, we can more easily back away from the

ledge and take purposeful action.

We've been working on our core values for over fifteen years now: living them, testing them, reordering them. So this process is not a *one and done, check the box, get your plaque on the wall* kind of deal. We are constantly feeling into our values and considering how best to use them in the future. Specificity of language in articulating our core values has refined this list to guide yearly vision statements and future goals.

Sometimes, depending on our life stage, we have to focus on one core value, and the others take a back seat. Sandi had to focus on gratitude before she could focus on her core values of wealth and freedom. That doesn't mean those values weren't present and important; they simply weren't driving the bus just yet.

Once you've identified your core values, it's a dance. You dance with each of them on a season-by-season basis. You develop an intrinsic trust that the dance will lead you where you need to be. Your core values will help communicate the next dance step.

KEY NUGGETS:

- Core values are the characteristics and traits that drive you.

- Core values and beliefs are similar but different in one important way: core values are intrinsic to who we are and ultimately don't change over time.

- One great way to uncover your core values is to notice where you have big emotions. Those usually point to a true core value.

- Core values and core wounds are interrelated but not the same.

- We can use our core values to notice when we are out of alignment, communicate effectively, make aligned decisions, and be seen, heard, and valued for who we are.

Chapter 7

YOUR PERSONAL SUPERPOWER

FUELING YOUR BLISS

Sandi: Finding My Wings

Stacie and I grew up alongside each other. We were just two years apart, and our siblings (Stephanie in 1982 and Ryan in 1989) came along much later. We depended on each other, and we looked to each other for guidance. Like many siblings, that sometimes meant we compared ourselves to the other.

While our parents never instilled a sense of competition between us, it's hard to avoid the comparison game. For me, as the younger of the two of us, I was always measuring myself against Stacie's yardstick. I saw that school was easy for Stacie, and it didn't feel easy for me. She whizzed through classes, and I was an average student. I felt like everyone loved her and doted over how good she was at "everything." I felt as if I couldn't measure up. So even in those situations where I stood out, showing everyone that I could do good things too, I still felt like I wasn't good enough. I turned to disassociating from the event, almost pretending I wasn't there so no one could really see me. As recently as a few years ago, I was still telling myself the story that I wasn't as smart as she was.

The truth was, I did well in some subjects and struggled in others. Even in the classes I did well in, I was constantly looking over my shoulder, convinced that I'd messed something up. When I was placed in advanced classes, I was afraid that someone was going to discover that I didn't belong. In my view, I skated by.

I landed in college in a pre-med program by the skin of my teeth. I'd written a very compelling college entrance essay about my knee injury from a ski accident that kept me from doing better in my junior year of high school. Thankfully, it bought me a few admission points. I was determined to put my nose to the grindstone, but a few semesters in, I was worn out and overwhelmed. I remember sitting around a table with my study group saying, "Where do you all put it? Because this brain is full." I knew I needed to make a shift. I switched majors several times and eventually graduated with a dual emphasis business degree in management and marketing.

My career was a similarly winding path. I worked as a recruiter, then in sales, and then chose real estate to make ends meet and be able to stay home with Hunter. It was through real estate in 2008 that I met Tony Hsieh, the late CEO of Zappos. I assisted Tony and his executive team with their commercial and residential real estate investments, helping them find the new Zappos headquarters when they wanted to move from Henderson, Nevada, to Downtown Las Vegas. The more I learned about Tony's philosophy on happiness, the way he reinvented corporate culture and supported his teams, the more inspired I was. Tony's book, *Delivering Happiness: A Path to Profits, Passion, and Purpose,* had recently been released, and he and his partner, Jenn Lim, launched Delivering Happiness, a culture consulting company based on the principles outlined in the book.

I had a deep knowing that I was meant to be a part of this greater purpose. I had been seeking something greater than myself my whole life. This just felt right. I knew this was it. I loved the message that Tony shared: focus on happiness and let your passion flow from there. I offered to volunteer or pitch in as they were getting the project off the ground. Before I knew it, I'd landed a job as the "Culture Operations Diva," running internal culture and operations.

I loved so much of my work there, but there were a few parts of the job I struggled with. The logistics and project management required for my role really tapped me. But the creative, innovative engagement and strategic development—those parts invigorated me!

I'd been volunteering in schools, helping to support school leaders to create culture shifts. I was passionate about supporting educators, and I loved taking what I'd learned from our work in corporate cultures to support the educational system. I decided, with Tony and Jenn's blessing and support, to leave my job with Delivering Happiness and to turn this volunteer work into a business. I launched a company focused on culture transformation within schools, originally Got Core Values, now called HumanizEDU.

Perhaps the most important direction on this journey to find my calling came a few years later. I'd become familiar with Roger Hamilton's work in creating Wealth Dynamics. Roger is a futurist, social entrepreneur, and the founder/CEO of The Genius Group, a global company at the forefront of the education revolution. I took his Wealth Dynamics assessment, which is a tool for finding your path of least resistance to success as an entrepreneur, for the first time in 2005. I listened to him describe the eight profiles/paths of least resistance to wealth, and I knew which profile I wanted to be. I thought I knew which one had the most value in the world. Unfortunately, that wasn't my profile. I remember being irritated, having a two-year-old temper tantrum inside my head and thinking, "But I don't want to be that." I couldn't see how my profile as a creator could possibly make any money—who needs ideas? Everyone has ideas, right? What I didn't realize was that the creator profile was more than just having ideas; it's the spark in the engine to get other people inspired and get things moving.

FOCUSING ON YOUR SUPERPOWER

Your superpower is like the supercharger to the engine. It is the thing that makes everything flow with ease and grace. Stacie can see that Sandi has a unique power to energize a group around a central idea. Sandi has honed her skill of being able to elicit that inner genius from other people—she is naturally adept at finding out what they're good at, what their desire or purpose is, and shining a light on it.

"She makes people feel good. She's just a magnet," Stacie says proudly. When Sandi was able to see how her unique skill set and power could galvanize the people around her to be their best selves, she could begin to rewrite her unconscious programming around not being good enough or smart enough.

We always think of this quote from Albert Einstein: *Everybody is a genius. But if you judge a fish by its ability to climb a tree, it will live its whole life believing that it is stupid.* When you learn what your natural brain-wired strength is, you lean into it. There is no need to compensate for the other things you may not excel in. Fish don't need to learn to climb trees; they simply need to be the best swimmers they can be. Squirrels can handle the tree climbing for them!

Turning on Your Superpower

Turning on your superpower is the super charge that makes any journey feel smooth. Activating your personal superpower is both simple and nuanced. Now that you've done the work to unpack your personal limiting beliefs, readjusted your lens on the world, given yourself permission to be true to you through your core values, and begun operating from a place of self-trust, you are primed to step into your personal power.

The first step is giving yourself permission to not be good at everything. That may be exhausting, not to mention impossible. And yet we often are taught or led to think that we need to be good at every subject, every sport, every elective instead of simply allowing ourselves to be superstars at some things and mediocre or—gasp!—bad at others. Rather than viewing this as failure, we can reframe it to see the ways we are built uniquely.

Our personal superpower is our natural brain-wired strength. You are likely quite aware of the things you don't excel at, but we challenge you to give yourself grace and permission to lean into the strengths that make you *you*. We believe that challenges can also be strengths (and vice versa), that there are two sides to every coin, and we simply have to acknowledge who we are to tap into our power.

We all have an inner genius, and it is our job to focus on what that genius is bringing to the world rather than try to compensate for what we might view as "weaknesses."

Sometimes compensating looks like false bravado or, on the other end of the spectrum, self-deprecating comments. For example, if I overemphasize my strengths with bravado, I'm insulating myself from your judgment. If I set the bar low by telling you that I'm no good at anything, you'll be really amazed when I achieve expectations. Compensation in these ways lets me off the hook and lowers outside expectations, allowing me to continue to move about in the world unseen and hiding my inner genius. Instead, we must shift to ownership of our weaknesses and things that can drain our energy, knowing that we are all navigating each day with our unique makeup of strengths and weaknesses.

When you are able to hold your weaknesses without a visceral charge, without beating yourself with the shame bat, you know that you're owning them. You speak about them matter-of-factly, and then leverage the superpowers of other people that supplement your superpower skill set.

Our culture has taught us that we "should" be good at everything. School culture feeds us these stories when we are young, and it is very hard to undo the damage. We "should" strive for excellence in every aspect of our lives. This reinforces an idea that success is not ever having to ask for help. But we are not islands. We need the support and assistance of others in order to exist and excel in the world. The more we fight against that, the more we get in our own way.

As a matter of fact, the more we are able to easily reach out for help, the more we can support each other. We are more adept at solving big problems when we are working together. When we are able to identify those times that we need help and ask for it without judgment or shame, it is then that the world will be filled with a lot more happy, healthy, whole humans.

Stacie: Embracing My Superpower

I failed my first hearing test in the fourth grade. I stood with my back turned toward the teacher administering the test, raising my hand when I heard the presented tones. I remember being questioned about my effort, fueling a core belief that I must always try harder. My hearing loss wasn't significant enough for me to need hearing aids. Due to my high frequency hearing loss, I began to pay close attention to people's mouths when they spoke, intuitively training myself to lip read. The funny thing is, my hearing loss really came in handy because I couldn't hear that high-pitched tone from our 1980s television, the one that signaled a need to replace the TV and that annoyed the heck out of everyone else. We never talked about my hearing loss in my family; it was just a fact of life.

When I was younger, I would often nod my head in agreement and smile, even though I wasn't fully comprehending everything that was happening. When I was a teenager, I would automatically say, "What?" or "Huh?" before even attempting to comprehend. "Stacie, pause and listen to what people are saying before you say 'huh,'" the adults in my life admonished.

I didn't feel comfortable or confident in scenarios where I couldn't predict what would be asked. I could put enough information together to give an answer based upon a set script. For example, when you go to a restaurant, you know they're going to ask initially what you want to drink. They're going to ask if you want an appetizer, then what you want for dinner. But if anyone were to ask me a question outside of that script, that would require me hearing them, and I was only hearing bits of information, not the whole conversation.

When I was younger, I felt like it made me appear less intelligent to say, "I can't hear you." Sandi often came to my rescue. She could tell the difference between the look on my face that said, "I don't understand" and the look that said, "I didn't hear that." She would say things a second time for me. We never talked about it; she just did it.

My hearing loss was never diagnosed, so there were no accommodations or any awareness of my situation. Because I sometimes didn't hear something and therefore did not respond, I was given the unbecoming nickname of Spacey Stacie by the adults in my world. This only increased my anxiety and hypervigilance.

On the flip side, my hearing loss created opportunities to develop other communication skills. I learned to read lips and watched people closely as they spoke. I developed a keen awareness of the disconnect between what someone is saying and what their eyes and facial expressions are communicating.

The next hearing test I received was in college, a screening before my summer work in a box factory. At that time, I was told I had a high frequency loss. But since no one speaks at those frequencies, there was nothing to be done. The technology at that time would only have provided aids that amplified all the sounds, not just those I was missing. Again, no one talked to me about advocating for myself to ensure adequate accommodations like sitting near the professor or positioning myself where I could easily see everyone in the classroom so I could see them as they spoke.

I relied on my own accommodations over the years. My kids learned to look in the rearview mirror when talking from the backseat. I would confirm reservation numbers or spellings of things by using C as in Charlie, S as in Sam, and E as in Edward. This is my way of accommodating for the high frequency hearing loss, which makes consonants within words challenging to identify.

In 2009, I returned to the audiologist, determined to find hearing aids that would help me hear high voices before beginning my internship as a school psychologist. The last thing I wanted was a little person in distress to have to repeat their story of trauma due to my hearing impairment. I was outfitted with the latest technology after a series of tests. During one particular test, I had to close my eyes (no lipreading allowed) and repeat individual words. The test revealed just how much I had been missing, amplifying my inability to comprehend individual words despite my best efforts. It brought me to tears, reinforcing the feeling that I wasn't "doing it right" or providing the correct answer, therefore appearing less intelligent.

During the COVID-19 pandemic, when individuals wore masks, my ability to hear and use my superpower of lipreading was further impeded. Communicating was a struggle. But it afforded me the opportunity again to practice advocating for myself by telling others that no matter how earnestly they looked from their eyes, I had no idea what they were saying if there was background noise and they were wearing a mask.

This became super evident when we took a trip in which we had to fly. On an airplane, there's such a high decibel of background noise that when someone speaks through a mask, it is very difficult for me to hear. I couldn't understand anything the flight attendant was saying. Although she had kind eyes and an expression that was meant to encourage understanding, I still couldn't hear her. But again, I was able to advocate for myself with the various flight attendants. Some individuals chose to lower their mask. Some chose to write things down. One flight attendant pulled up a picture of beer or wine to ask if I wanted a drink.

I've grown into a place where I can freely talk about my hearing impairment. In fact, I love to talk about the advanced technologies in hearing aids. I use my struggles to relate to others. I advocate for myself in an attempt to model talking about needs and struggles openly. I often say, "I'm hearing impaired. If I answer your question in a way that doesn't make sense, it's probably because I misheard you." By openly stating this and advocating for myself, I no longer worry about others perceiving me as less intelligent or as not paying attention.

While the world once embraced the terminology "hard of hearing," I've personally preferred to identify as hearing impaired. Hearing isn't something I can improve by trying harder or practicing to do better. It's simply part of my unique makeup. Now that I've grown to embrace this part of myself, it has become emblematic of my desire to make sure everyone has a voice and a space to be heard. The superpower of acknowledging and creating a safe space for all aspects of verbal communication and nonverbal expression is embedded in my work as a psychologist, as well as in every fiber of my life.

LET GO OF THE GRIND MINDSET

The grind is a lie. Our culture has adopted the narrative, "I have to work hard before I can get to that place of ease." That is simply not true. How many times have you heard successful individuals talk about how they worked so hard for so long, and now they've reached a point where they are doing what they love—they are in love with their lives—and they wish they had found this ease sooner? Well, we can all do that!

Would you believe it if we told you that life could be easy? We are taught to believe that achieving and acquiring things in life has to be hard work. There is so much language to this effect that permeates our consciousness: grind, hustle, make it happen, work hard, etc., etc.

When we insist that we must grind, we are actually stepping out of the flow.

We've spent several chapters examining and releasing our own personal limiting stories. Now it's time to address the collective narratives that don't serve us. We've been programmed to believe that we are rewarded for hard work *and* that if we aren't working hard, we are lazy. In reality, if you are living by your natural brain-wired strengths, life doesn't feel like work. We have to step out of that mainstream mindset and be willing to embrace a new paradigm.

Accepting and celebrating our superpower is the ultimate act of self-love. We are accepting ourselves for who we are instead of beating ourselves with the shame bat for who we aren't.

Likely, your superpower is something that rides very close to the surface and only requires a bit of reflection to see.

When do you feel most in flow? Said another way, when are you so engrossed in what you're doing that you don't notice time passing? When does *doing* feel more like *being*? This is your biggest clue. When you feel at ease, when you don't notice the minutes ticking by because you're enthralled with what you're doing—you've tapped into your superpower.

SANDI: INTEGRATING MY SUPERPOWER

I'd followed Roger Hamilton's career, and I'd even been a speaker-wrangler at one of his events in Vegas. I was going on a women's retreat to Bali in the spring of 2015 and saw that Roger was going to be there at the same time, so I reached out. He invited me to stay at Vision Villas and join the training they were offering. I took the plunge. A friend gifted me the money to attend, so I extended my trip, and the rest is history.

Roger invited me to be part of the Crystal Circle group when I was there. He instructed anyone who wanted to learn more about the group to come to a special breakfast in the morning. I went to breakfast, sat down in the sun, and he sat down next to me and said, "Are you going to be okay in the light?"

"Yeah, I'm fine," I replied. The symbolism of the moment didn't dawn on me until later.

I had a free day on my last day in Bali. Roger suggested I climb to the top of one of their volcanoes, so I did. I hired a guide, packed a backpack, and off I went at two in the morning. The goal was to reach the top by sunrise and have breakfast at the peak. I was not really equipped for this kind of hike. All I had were my tennis shoes. Thankfully, a full moon helped light the way as we hiked through the night. My excitement was much more enthusiastic than my endurance, and I had to stop several times as we climbed the slippery shale volcanic rocks. I played it off a few times, soaking in the beauty of the moonlit night. As we neared the summit, my guide, Jarro, offered to carry my pack (because I'd packed like I was going for six days instead of six hours!) and reached down to help me so we could make it by sunrise. As he grasped my hand, I had an epiphany: I had to be willing to ask for help in order to fully step into my power.

I leaned in to being mentored by Roger and becoming part of this global community of entrepreneurs all learning together, and my whole life changed. I came back with the system of Talent Dynamics to be able to share with our schools. I was recognizing my worth in the world in a whole new way. And I'd opened up to the knowledge that I don't have to do it all on my own. The wisdom of my superpower can create the holistic vision of wealth I dream of.

UNCOVERING YOUR NATURAL BRAIN-WIRED STRENGTH

As we shared earlier, Sandi was first exposed to Roger Hamilton's work in 2005 through his Wealth Dynamics Assessment. The ideas that underpin Wealth Dynamics became the framework for Talent Dynamics,[12] which helps leaders tap into their strengths and the strengths of their teams to build healthy organizations. These systems are rooted in archetypes developed by Carl Jung and the five-thousand-year-old

---

12   "Talent Dynamics Profile Test," HumanizEDU, https://humanizedu.com/talent-dynamics.

Chinese system of thinking called the I-Ching.

Traditional Chinese philosophers used the study of the Five Elements to explain a wide range of phenomena, from weather and space concepts to internal medicine to how the human mind works. The study of Chinese energy is central to many Eastern philosophies and academic pursuits from design to medicine.

Talent Dynamics introduces the Five Elements/Frequencies to model how our brains work. Each Element is linked to specific natural strengths that can help you find your personal flow. The more we step into our natural flow, the more we can amplify our aligned leadership skills, embrace the value we naturally bring to the world, and learn how to effectively communicate with those around us. Each element relates to both positive and challenging personal traits, an example of Yin and Yang. As you develop a deeper understanding of your inner self within the Five Elements, you'll learn valuable information about how you are "wired." You'll discover what drives your energy, and on the flip side, you'll learn about the kinds of activities that seem to drain your motivation and energy.

These Elements are referred to as Frequencies. When you consider how our brains receive and process information, it's easy to think of the energy waves as frequencies. These Frequencies are also connected to the way we learn.

THE FIVE ELEMENTS/FREQUENCIES (TALENT DYNAMICS)

Wood (Dynamo) relates to innovation and big picture thinking.

Fire (Blaze) relates to extroverted energy with a focus on people.

Earth (Tempo) relates to sensory energy and deep-rooted service.

Metal (Steel) relates to systems-based thinking, gaining energy from more introverted activities.

Water (Spirit) relates to the overall *why* behind everything and how things grow and flow naturally.

When we learn what our dominant frequency is and begin to work with it instead of focusing on how to improve the areas in our personalities that we view as deficient, we are stepping into flow.

You can learn more about this system and others in the resources section of the book.

APPLYING THE SYSTEM

One part of putting the Talent Dynamics system into practice is developing conscious communication. When we are able to identify how the key people in our life operate, we can hone our communication and connection skills. Sandi notices the language people use when they ask questions. Stacie often asks questions that begin with the word *How,* which indicates that she is a steel-dominant frequency and that she is a systems thinker. She focuses on how to make something happen and how to replicate it with ease. Sandi asks questions that begin with the operative word *What.* She is a big picture thinker who excels at getting things started. She is always thinking: *What if?*

Those who begin their questions with *Who* like to connect. They tend to be more extroverted and find joy in bringing people together. Those who tend toward the *When* and the *Where* are the logistics people in the crowd, or the tempo-dominant frequency. They work best organizing details.

When you begin learning to identify your own superpower and step into that flow, you'll find that you are more invested in facilitating that for others. We can support our families, friends, and teams to step into their own superpowers. Imagine the beauty of a group of people all existing in alignment and flow!

Sandi knows that when she's asking Stacie a question, it's easiest for Stacie to process if she begins the question with *How.* If she opens the conversation with a word that Stacie's brain doesn't have to translate, they are more likely to step right into the stream of connection. This is especially important when we are in more challenging situations. If we're able to step in the stream of connection, a challenging conversation can feel fruitful instead of adversarial.

When we are modeling living in this way, we are inspiring and influencing those around us to do the same.

SANDI: EVOLVING AWARENESS OF MY SUPERPOWER

We are all learning all the time, and our consciousness is constantly evolving. Just when we think we've got it all figured out, one of those pesky old patterns or beliefs—personal or cultural—sneaks up on us.

A decade ago, Stacie and I were preparing to present our first talk together at the Supporting the Emotional Needs of Gifted Children conference. Our talk was entitled *Gifted Siblings: The Good, Bad, and Ugly*.

"Yeah, but you know I'm not gifted, right?" I asked. Stacie looked at me incredulously.

"What are you talking about? You were in GATE, right?"

"Yeah," I replied. I recognized that I had been in the GATE program in elementary school. Once each week a handful of kids were pulled out of class to do extracurricular activities.

"The Gifted And Talented Education program?" Stacie said, waiting for the lightbulb to go on.

"I thought that was just a fun elective," I said, laughing a little.

Thirty years later, I still had no idea why I'd been placed in the program. Even though I had "proof" that I had exceptional levels of intelligence, I still felt like I'd pulled the wool over someone's eyes.

I was still up against those old patterns and limiting beliefs. It continues to be an evolution, but now that I know in my bones about my strength, it's just about getting the old stuff unstuck." It began to sink in that perhaps I was a "gifted and talented" person after all.

I continue to give myself permission to be and celebrate who I uniquely am, knowing that I don't have to be good at everything. I can lean into doing things in ways that come easily and give me energy rather than forcing myself to do everything all at once by myself. Each step on the journey continues to be a recalibration and celebration of the small wins, igniting my unique inner genius.

KEY NUGGETS:

- ‿ Hustle Culture is a myth. We don't have to grind! This is a collective narrative we'd like to unpack.

- ‿ By stepping into your natural brain-wired strength—or superpower—you will find that life feels more in flow, and you don't need to hustle.

- ‿ There are a number of ways to uncover your superpower, but you can tap into one through assessments like Talent Dynamics.

Chapter 8

BUILDING CONNECTION

YOUR FELLOW TRAVELERS

Just as we sat down to compose this chapter in September 2022, Hurricane Ian ripped through southwestern Florida, right through the communities where Stacie lives and works. Sandi waited thirty-six hours on pins and needles for news of Stacie's wellbeing. The storm subsided, and Stacie let everyone know that she, her family, and home were safe and sound. Then the work began. Stacie and her team worked to bring their therapy practice back online. Concurrently, she began to share ways for parents to talk to their children about the aftermath of the storm, and she connected with educators about how to support children and families in the classroom.

In the aftermath of disaster, communities come together. People work together to get those directly impacted the services and resources they need, and everyone pitches in to rebuild infrastructure. But when the acute threat has subsided, the threads that tie everyone together begin to fray.

After Hurricane Ian, lots of people pitched in to clean up. After a few weeks, though, everyone seemed to go back to business as usual. Yet, there was still a residual need. Many people were still navigating rebuilding their homes and reestablishing their roots, but the predominant feeling was that the cleanup effort was over.

On top of that, the community hadn't had a chance to tend to the emotional trauma that the storm created. A few weeks after the hurricane, a normal thunderstorm moved through the area. Stacie could feel her anxiety rise as the wind rattled the windows once again, hearkening back to the ten hours of listening to the wind beat against houses a few weeks prior. When she mentioned this to a group of colleagues the next day, they echoed her feelings of anxiousness, opening a door of opportunity to talk about the longer-lasting effects of enduring a natural disaster. By making space to begin to collectively heal those wounds, we are then better able to show up for our community.

One of the consequences of not giving ourselves permission to feel the heartbreak and pain of a traumatic event is that we don't make space for those around us to do so either. Stacie worried about students returning to a "business as usual" attitude at school. She feared that some teachers may blow by the processing of the tragic event. It's easier to control adhering to the arithmetic lesson plan than it is to go off book and talk about feelings. We are often afraid to open up the vault of our own emotions because we're afraid they're too big, too powerful. What if we start crying and don't stop?

(**Side note**: Sandi's therapist once told her, lovingly, "You won't cry forever." She was right.)

In this chapter, we're going to turn our lens outward a bit. Now that we've learned how to nurture and develop our own psyches in a caring, radically responsible way, we're going to explore our hardwired need for connection and belonging. When we care for our own needs and show up as our authentic selves, we can, in turn, develop and nurture our communities.

HARDWIRED FOR CONNECTION

There has been a proliferation of memes on social media in the last few years that glorify reclusion. There have been a lot of "I don't even like people" or "I don't need anyone but my cat" posts circulating. It's as if in order to cope with the pandemic isolation, people leaned into this misanthropic isolation. These memes cite introversion as the root of their reclusive antics, but they are mischaracterizing this whole subset of people. We all need people. Introverts need smaller numbers and more time to recover, but they still require human connection.

We suspect this is connected to the very American ideal of individualism. There is a myth of pulling oneself up by the bootstraps, as though relying only on ourselves shows strength. In reality, that way of being has gotten us to a very disjointed, disconnected place, and we're suffering as a result.

Being connected to one another is a survival mechanism. Hundreds of thousands of years ago, it was critical to our survival to travel in packs. Being alone was a first-class ticket to getting eaten by a saber-toothed tiger, attacked by a different tribe, or starving to death. As a result, we developed a hardwired sense that we have to find our group in order to protect ourselves and thrive. This is not unique to humans, obviously. Many, many species of mammals travel together in groups for the same reasons.

As we evolved, things got a little more complicated. We had to begin to define our pack. Who gets to be part of it? Is it the people who live near me? Those who look like me? Is it someone who believes the same things I do? Who enjoys what I enjoy? Who roots for the same football team on Sunday afternoons? Are my pack members those who share my DNA?

The thing is, research shows that having a social network is not just a survival mechanism, it is what helps us thrive. It increases our happiness quotients, reduces stress, and increases our health outcomes.

FINDING COMMUNITY VS. FITTING IN

We've spent the last seven chapters digging into how to give yourself permission to authentically be yourself and let that guide you to a more blissful life. Being in community with people who see and hear you for your beautiful, unadorned self is critical to finding that rhythm of happiness. We seek authentic belonging, the experience of being part of a community in which we can show up as our whole selves without fear of judgment, or worse: ostracization. Being included in a community in which you have to armor or shield yourself in order to be present isn't authentic belonging. What's more, it may lead to shutting down, withdrawing, and playing small.

There will undoubtedly be circumstances in which we have to withhold or shelter parts of ourselves for our safety or for the comfort of others. We like to think of this as the circles of safety. Your innermost circle consists of those with whom you can share every bit of yourself: the good, bad, and ugly. One ring out are those with whom you trust your wellbeing but perhaps don't share your inner soul with. One ring out from that are those individuals who feed certain parts of your life but don't get access to the full you. A ring out beyond that might be the acquaintances in your orbit. Knowing who gets to be in those circles is an exercise in boundary setting and self-care.

CIRCLES OF SAFETY

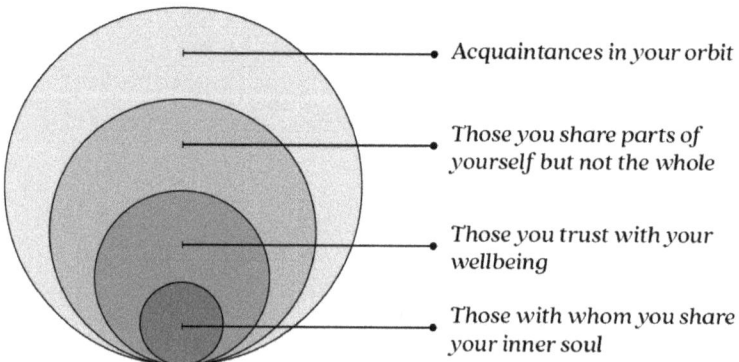

- Acquaintances in your orbit
- Those you share parts of yourself but not the whole
- Those you trust with your wellbeing
- Those with whom you share your inner soul

While that innermost circle is critically important, *all* of those rings build our connection and community. The litmus test for a healthy community is that you are able to show up with healthy boundaries as yourself and be welcomed. You need not justify or apologize but can be as you are in each moment.

ATTACHMENT STYLES

One way to examine the ways we form relationships and therefore community is to consider our attachment styles. Initially, researchers assumed that our attachment styles were a result of our upbringing; the way we attached depended on how we were cared for as babies. If your parents were available and responsive to your needs, you developed a *secure attachment* style. If your caregivers were inconsistent, you would develop an *anxious attachment* style, and if your parents or caregivers were unresponsive or distant, you would develop an *avoidant attachment* style. Current research, including in-depth examination by Dr. Amir Levine and Rachel S.F. Heller in their book, *Attached. The New Science of Adult Attachment and How it Can Help You Find—and Keep—Love,* tells us that our attachment style is formed through a variety of factors, including our parents' style of caregiving, social factors, and life experiences.[13]

It's important to know this: dependency is not a bad thing! In our hyper-individualistic society, we are often taught to believe that depending on someone else makes us weak. As recently as the 1940s, new parents were taught to not spend too much time with their infants, as this could result in emotionally unhealthy adults. Children and parents were kept separate in hospitals for fear of creating needy, insecure children.

---

13   Amir Levine and Rachel Heller, Attached. *The New Science of Adult Attachment and How It Can Help You Find—And Keep—Love* (TarcherPerigree, 2011).

The codependency movement told us that we should not depend on others for our comfort or happiness; our wellbeing is our own responsibility. Being too enmeshed in another person was said to be maladaptive; we needed boundaries to be healthy. While there is some truth to this in certain circumstances, it's also important to note that in healthy relationships, attachment is actually good for us.

In fact, numerous studies show that when we form attachments to another person, we physiologically connect to each other. Our partner's presence can help regulate our blood pressure, our heart rate, breathing, and hormone levels in our blood. From a biological perspective, dependency is a fact, not a choice or preference.

Those with a *secure attachment style* feel comfortable with intimacy and are warm and loving. Individuals with an *anxious attachment style* crave closeness and tend to worry about their partner's ability to love them. *Avoidant attachment* styles equate intimacy with a loss of freedom and tend to minimize closeness. The fourth style is an *anxious avoidant or disorganized attachment,* which is characterized by traits of both styles.

None of these behaviors are unhealthy—they are simply the way we are built.

Understanding where we fall in these categories can provide us with information to help navigate our relationship patterns. Knowledge is power: if you recognize your tendencies, you are more able to navigate the winding road of building relationships and community. Moreover, as we've discussed, our brains love patterns. So as we develop, we learn to look for patterns and learn from them. Having a bit of language and a label to understand our way of interacting with the world around us can help us be more conscious and intentional in our choices.

COREGULATION

Have you ever had that experience where you're super amped up from something that happened at work, and when you get home, your partner's calm, easy demeanor seems to be a tonic for your frazzled soul? There's a name for that: *coregulation*. Essentially, coregulation is the way that the nervous system of one person influences another. When one person is out of sorts (or, in psychology-speak, dysregulated) and isn't able to self-regulate, often coregulation helps ease them back into a state of peace. We explored self-regulation in Chapter 5, but let's explore how we can support one another by coregulating. Coregulation *supports* self-regulation, which is the greatest skill in our tote bag to assist in navigating our uncertain path.

Sandi: Practicing Coregulation

After I moved across the country, I felt a bit frazzled. My nervous system was in overdrive, and I began to employ all the tools at my fingertips to take care of myself: exercise, meditation, journaling. While those tools are usually an express ticket to finding my peace, this time they weren't working. I still felt off, so I called Stacie.

She was able to listen to my distress and reminded me to give myself permission to slow down. Stacie mirrored back to me that I was navigating a heck of a lot, and that it was okay to clear my calendar and take some time to come back to myself. Stacie's calming presence helped me to take the additional steps necessary to self-regulate.

☙

How does this apply in a larger context? You've been learning tools of self-awareness and advocacy throughout this book. As you become more aware of yourself and the way you are showing up in the world, you'll become aware of how you are impacting the world around you. We all carry an energy with us wherever we go. When we are aware of it and cognizant of how it might impact others, we are consciously creating the best scenario for ourselves, our partners, families, colleagues, and communities.

None of us are islands, and the way we interact and are reflected in our various communities contributes to the way we view ourselves and how we behave in groups.

STACIE: FINDING BELONGING

As I shared before, I stood out in my family. I grew up with my mom, who is Caucasian, and my two light-complected, light-haired sisters. I had dark hair and eyes and brown skin. I heard a constant running commentary, mostly from adults, trying to explain this. *You must look like your dad.* As I got older, I was often asked where I was from. I learned to counter the question with, "Are you asking where I was born, where I grew up, or my ethnicity?" Nine times out of ten, they were asking about my ethnicity.

When I was younger, to answer the "Where are you from?" question, I would say, "California."

"But what are you?"

Eventually, people began to ask what my ethnicity was. I'd tell them that my grandparents were from Mexico. This seemed to put their minds at ease: *Oh, you're Mexican American.*

My junior year of college, as I shared before, I studied abroad in Russia. It was the early 1990s, just after the fall of the Soviet Union, so it was a unique time to be in the country. At that time, Americans were still very idealized. While I was there, people often queried the same things.

"Where are you from?"

"I'm from the US."

"No, no . . . where are you from?"

"I have a United States passport," I'd reply. They'd make an incredulous face, like they weren't sure. "I am a United States citizen. I was born on the United States Air Force base on the Azores. Both my parents are US citizens."

More skepticism. "What's your heritage?"

Finally, I would have to say, "My grandmother is from Mexico."

"Ah, so you are Mexican."

It was enough to make me want to pull my hair out. It consistently left me feeling out of place and not fitting into a category or belonging to one specific community.

I got my undergraduate degree at Occidental College in Los Angeles. There was a large population of Hispanic students, but I didn't fit in with them either. I was raised mostly by my mother, and she wasn't Mexican. So I didn't grow up hearing the language spoken from birth. Mexican traditions were not embedded in everything we did.

I didn't fit into the Caucasian American box. I didn't fit into the Hispanic box. Where did I belong?

As a woman, I always felt just outside the circle as well. When I was a sophomore in college, I worked the midnight shift at a box factory alongside thirty-five men. I was the only woman. My grandfather worked the morning shift, so I was not just a woman, but a granddaughter. No one quite knew what jobs to assign me. As an adult, I've always been very driven. That isn't always appreciated in females. As I've built my business, I've often heard people refer to me as ambitious in a tone that made it clear that they weren't issuing a compliment. Ambitious became synonymous with unapproachable.

Recently, I mentioned that I was applying for a grant for minority business owners through the local chamber of commerce. My friend looked at me blankly and then said, "I just never see you as a minority." I wasn't quite sure what to make of that. I suppose I'd just like to be with people who fully see me. So I've always felt a little like *the other*.

When I turned forty, I told my mother and father that I wanted to return to my birthplace for my fiftieth birthday. I wanted to have the experience of returning to my origins with them by my side. They'd be divorced for over forty years, and it might be uncomfortable, but it was important to me. I didn't give them any option. I just told them, "Look, this is happening."

In the summer of 2022, we made it happen. My whole family was there with me in the Azores. As we toured the islands, I had the chance to share the deeper reason behind the trip with some of the locals. They threw their arms open as if I were a long-lost daughter. No one asked me to qualify where I was from or what my ethnicity was. I didn't need to explain anymore. It was as if I was accepted just because I was born on that soil. "You're Azorean!" they exclaimed.

Every time someone asks me, *What are you? What are you really?* I want to answer, "I'm a really good person," and leave it at that.

My spiritual belief and one of my core values is that we are all One. There is no hierarchy to our existence; we're all part of the grander universe. It is this oneness, this looking for similarities rather than differences, that is the linchpin of how I build community. When I view every human as part of my community, it's much easier to let go of the urge to fit in and instead joyfully nurture a strong sense of belonging.

DEVELOPING YOUR FRAMILY

In *The Gifts of Imperfection*, Brené Brown reminds us that, "Connection is the energy that exists between people when they feel seen, heard, and valued."[14] When we feel fed and nurtured by our relationships and not judged, we can show up with our full selves—beautiful imperfections and all.

We are incredibly lucky that our sisterhood is a wondrous haven of belonging for both of us. We also recognize that not all families allow that safe space. Because we are hardwired to connect, it's important to build relationships with people who will provide the open-hearted care we seek. We have a name for those friends, intimate partners, or roommates—the Framily (friends + family).

Who in your life fits into that circle of love and belonging?

---

14   Brené Brown, *The Gifts of Imperfection: 10th Anniversary Edition* (Simon & Schuster, 2022).

Writer, traveling teacher, and activist Dr. Parker Palmer has written extensively on building communities. He identifies what he calls "the divided life" as a personal pathology, something that keeps us from wholeness. The divided life separates us from our souls, hiding our true identity for fear of exposure. The divided life puts us in a position of defensiveness, of being steeped in imposter syndrome. When we seek to integrate our lives, we can show up fully as ourselves. This book has been walking you through the steps so you can return to your bliss. Palmer asserts that this is a critical step in building community.

If we aren't able to show up as our full, integrated selves, then are the families or communities to which we belong the places where we can be authentic? Is the connection real if we aren't bringing our whole selves to the table?

> In this culture, we know how to create spaces that invite the intellect to show up, analyzing reality, parsing logic, and arguing its case... We know how to create spaces that invite the emotions into play, reacting to injury, expressing anger or joy ... We know how to create spaces that invite the will to show up, consolidating effort and energy on behalf of a shared task ... And we surely know how to create spaces that invite the ego to put in an appearance, polishing its image, protecting its turf and demanding its rights ... But we seem to know very little about creating spaces that invite the soul to show, to make itself known.[15]

Palmer has created principles for what he calls *Circles of Trust*, or spaces where individuals can connect, learn, and grow together.

1. **Give and receive welcome.** Foster a spirit of hospitality.

2. **Be present.** Acknowledge your doubts, fears, and failings as well as your convictions, joys, and successes.

---

15   Parker J. Palmer, *A Hidden Wholeness: The Journey Toward an Undivided Life* (Wiley, 2022).

3. **What is offered is by invitation, not demand.** Share if you choose, but never feel obligated. Do what your soul calls for and know you do it with support.

4. **Speak your truth in ways that respect others' truths.** Our views of reality may differ, but speaking one's truth in a circle of trust does not mean interpreting, correcting, or debating what others say. Speak from your center to the center of the circle using "I" statements, trusting people to do their own sifting and winnowing.

5. **No fixing, saving, advising, or correcting.**

6. **Learn to respond to others with open questions.** Do not respond with counsel or corrections. Using honest, open questions helps us hear each other into deeper speech.

7. **When the going gets tough, turn to wonder.** Turn from reaction and judgment to wonder and compassionate inquiry. Set aside judgment to listen to others—and to yourself—more deeply.

8. **Attend to your own inner teacher.** We learn from others, of course. But as we explore poems, stories, questions, and silence in a circle of trust, we have a special opportunity to learn from within. Pay close attention to your own reactions and responses, to your most important teacher.

9. **Trust and learn from silence.** Silence is a gift in a noisy world and a way of knowing in itself. Treat silence as a member of the group. After someone has spoken, take time to reflect without immediately filling the space with words.

10. **Observe deep confidentiality.**

11. **Know that it is possible to leave the circle with whatever it was you needed when you arrived and that the seeds planted here**

can keep growing in the days ahead.[16]

Do your communities foster any or all of these principles? What would it be like if they did? What if we built our communities like circles of trust? How would this change how we react to crisis, pain, or heartbreak? How can you continue to build a circle of trust in your own family?

SANDI: OUR SISTER CONNECTION

While Stacie was navigating the breakup of her first marriage, embarking upon an unconventional education journey, and marrying the rock-solid man who is now her husband, I was shaking things up in Vegas. My career was unfolding in a way that I didn't expect while finding my way through my first marriage and divorce. Through all of it, we remained a supportive sister unit. However, we weren't having meaningful sister conversations about the topics you're reading about in this book.

While Stacie was studying psychology and multiple modalities of thinking, she was also a spiritual seeker. This created a perfect storm of wisdom. I was learning from a variety of thought leaders and spiritual teachers, traveling internationally, and forming my own new thought patterns and beliefs. We were both busy with our careers, our families, and living on different coasts, which meant deep conversations about these topics just never happened.

The deepest friendships are able to rekindle with the simplest spark despite the friends being apart, even after years apart, and so ours did too. It was a bit like discovering each other all over again.

We had grown up in the Catholic faith, but over the years we'd each found that certain aspects of the religion no longer resonated. Independently we had begun to search for other ways to fulfill our

---

16   Center for Courage & Renewal, accessed November 16, 2022, https://couragerenewal.org.

spiritual life. I took a life-changing trip to Bali and was exploring big questions about God and the Universe, learning about body awareness and somatic healing. Meanwhile, Stacie had been exploring the Unity Church and was drawn in by its implementation of positive psychology principles, self-reflection, and introspection.

One weekend while I was visiting Stacie in Florida, she invited me to accompany her and her family to church. I was familiar with the church—after all, Reverend Patricia Reiter had married Stacie and Roland in 2013. While I didn't feel drawn to organized religion, I respected and celebrated Stacie's spiritual home and was happy to participate. So there we were, after the service, waiting for Roland to finish helping with the AV equipment, and we decided to take a peek in the church bookstore. As we wandered the aisles, we began pointing out titles. Stacie gestured to Brené Brown's *Rising Strong*.

"Our congregation is reading this together," she said.

"You are? I'm reading that right now!" I picked up Deepak Chopra's *The Ultimate Happiness Prescription*. "Have you read this? It's such a good companion piece."

Our energy was building. Suddenly, we were comparing notes on Louise Hay's *You Can Heal Your Life* and Wayne Dyer's *Change Your Thoughts—Change Your Life: Living The Wisdom of The Tao*. We realized how we'd been on parallel paths of exploring spirituality for years and just didn't realize how close we had been this whole time.

This discovery of commonality was like hitting the sister jackpot. We had always had an unshakable bond: we had depended on each other growing up and had been each other's biggest cheerleaders. We were always just a phone call or a plane ride away. Realizing after all these years of parenting and working and learning in our own worlds that, in fact, our spiritual selves overlapped in this way was like having the sun peek out from behind clouds. This realization was where this book was born.

We all want to be seen and heard and witnessed for all that we are. We desire to be known and accepted, not for what we bring to the table, but for our simple existence. Our sisterhood had always been built around those pillars of belonging. But the thread of a similar belief system cemented what has become a beautiful partnership. We believe that this is not just possible, but within reach of every single one of you.

STEPHANIE: MY PATH TO BLISS

Stacie was turning fifty, and I was turning forty on the same day, so of course, we decided to celebrate together. Sandi surprised us with a whole beautiful weekend at a fancy hotel and spa in Austin so we could be pampered and celebrated.

The weekend was pretty amazing. It felt like something was shifting for me. First of all, the fact that all these people—my sisters, my husband who helped orchestrate the whole thing—loved me enough to do something this special felt really incredible. The hotel and the spa were, just, wow! I think the best part of the whole weekend was sitting around in our suite, drinking wine and talking.

I always looked at my sisters and thought, *they're perfect.* They had perfect lives. Their dad was involved and did all the dad things, whereas my dad was absent at best. I remember when I was a tiny kid, I was acting out, and someone told my mom, "She acts like that because of who she came from." *I was behaving poorly because I came from my dad, who was rotten.* After that, I just believed that I was bad too. My sisters were good, and I wasn't. So I shielded myself from them, or maybe I shielded them from me.

I never really considered the fact that they had dealt with trauma too. I had trauma because of my upbringing, but my dad and mom were together for years before I came along. Stacie and Sandi dealt with all that for all those years. We talked this through during our weekend together, and I felt like something was changing a little.

A couple months later, I had a terrible car accident. JJ, my husband,

and I were on our way to work one morning when a car hit us on the freeway and shoved us into an embankment and a guardrail. We were lucky to be alive. That experience changed my life forever.

I had a variety of injuries, including being partially paralyzed. I had to have back surgery and ankle surgery. JJ fared a little better. I still have nightmares, though.

After we got home from the emergency room, we got a knock at the door. JJ answered it. It was a woman from a nearby church. He told her it wasn't a good time; we had just been in a bad car accident. She just looked at us and said, "You are so lucky neither of you died. I need to say a prayer for you." She prayed for us, which was nice, though I'm not really into all that. The thing is, it hadn't occurred to either of us that we could have died. There was no reason that the car hadn't flipped over and killed one or both of us.

We had been so busy, having just moved to the Austin area. We were working long hours, taking care of the kids, always going, going, going. I think the accident was a message from the universe saying, "Stop, pause, and look around. Is this the life you want?"

When we talked about the accident, we were so grateful we were alive and that we weren't more seriously hurt. We were lucky! Instead of looking at it as this terrible thing that happened to us, we began to realize how lucky we were. That's a whole shift. That was the universe's message. We needed to listen. The universe could have been a little more gentle, but it happened. Here we are.

I am a different person than I was five years ago. I am a different person than I was seven months ago. I am constantly getting better, and I realize now that I wasn't a bad person before. I am constantly becoming more self-aware and accepting myself, flaws, wrinkles, saggy butt cheeks, and all. Sometimes I cycle backward and want to curl up in my bed and cry and watch Hallmark movies. But that's okay. I feel it, and then I get up and move on.

I'm letting my sisters in more. Acknowledging that I'm not bad and that they had it rough too helped the walls come down. They love me regardless of where I've been or who I come from. That has been, well, pretty amazing.

If I could say anything to people in my shoes, it would be simply to stop and breathe. If you are as stubborn as I was about not letting people in, just stop. Stop and breathe, remember the good things in your life and the people who surround you with love. Listen to them. Are you annoyed with those people in your life? Well, try to love them back and let them in. I was annoyed with Stacie and Sandi because I didn't want to disappoint them. I didn't think I was worthy of it. But we are. And I am.

KEY NUGGETS:

- ﹏ All humans are wired to connect.
- ﹏ We can be intentional about with whom and how we build our connections through creating circles of safety.
- ﹏ As we build our communities, using intentional practices of connection can go a long way in building circles of trust.

Chapter 9

OWNING YOUR BLISS

YOUR PATH IS PAVED WITH JOYFUL BLISS

While joy is a positive emotion linked to pleasurable experiences and a sense of contentment, bliss is a more profound and enduring state that often involves a deeper connection with oneself, others, or the divine.

When was the last time you experienced pure joy? When was the last time you laughed out loud? When was the last time you exuded bliss? Close your eyes for a moment and travel back to that moment. What was the temperature like? What was going on around you? What did you hear and see? Where were you? Now, notice what's going on in your body. What are your muscles in your face doing—are they tense or relaxed? What sensations do you feel—is your heart beating faster; is your breathing slower? Are your shoulders sliding down from your ears? If you tell the story of that moment, what does your voice sound like? What does joy feel like?

STACIE: VENICE/FLORIDA

My husband and I and our adult children traveled to Italy in December 2021. While the pandemic restrictions had been lifted, the way in which we traveled in this new COVID-19 landscape made the trip slightly more stressful than it might normally have been. There were more hoops to jump through and more precautions to take to make sure everyone was safe. Regardless of the limitations, the trip was a glorious one for the whole family.

When I returned home, people asked, "What was your favorite part?" The first memory that came to mind was dining at Florida, the restaurant. We live in Venice, Florida, so the synchronicity of finding a restaurant called Florida in Venice, Italy, was hilarious and thrilling. The whole entourage was delighted. We sat outdoors, of course, right on the canal.

"One of my core values is togetherness, and here we were, together in this beautiful place," I recalled. "I love eating outside, I love being near water, and having all these things lined up was just perfect." That moment, while sitting at that Venice restaurant, I watched my children tease each other and laugh together. The winter breeze and the gondola drifted by, and as we sipped Chianti, I thought, *This is pure bliss.*

⚛

If you can't recall a moment of joy or profound bliss, that's okay. Sometimes it's hard to recall something from which we've been distanced. Also, when we haven't had a chance to absorb a feeling, it's hard to remember what it feels like. There's nothing wrong with you. Part of our cultural programming is to speed through these micro moments— both moments of extreme happiness and those of sadness or grief. We are taught to move on to the next thing, that the speed at which we reach the outcome is what will make us successful.

Over the course of this book, we've invited you to slow down and notice your patterns, beliefs, feelings, and reactions. We've asked you to be intentional about observing yourself with care, compassion, and radical accountability. That's taken a lot of effort!

In this chapter, we're again asking you to slow down, and this time, we want you to notice the moments of joyousness. If we apply the same principles we have throughout the book—noticing, curiously inquiring, and taking aligned action—then we can lovingly witness and own our bliss.

AUTHENTIC BLISS VS. PROGRAMMING

Perhaps the first step in the process of noticing your joy is to acknowledge that your blissful moments are unique and may not be the ones your family, friends, or community lift up as joyous moments. We are programmed to find bliss in big moments: our wedding day, holidays, our child's first birthday. But in reality, sometimes those massive landmark moments are also fraught with anxiety, expectations, and even grief.

Sometimes, the most blissful experiences are in the ordinary moments in our day. When we begin to notice these moments, we can begin to build our stockpile of joy and bliss.

LEVELS OF HAPPINESS

In *Delivering Happiness,* Tony Hsieh outlines a Happiness Framework that cultivates **Pleasure, Passion,** and **Higher Purpose**. [17]

> The pleasure type of happiness is about always chasing the next high. I like to refer to it as the 'Rock Star' type of happiness because it's great if you can have a constant inflow of stimuli, but it's very hard to maintain unless you're living the lifestyle of a rockstar. Research shows that this type of happiness has the shortest

---

17   Tony Hsieh , *Delivering Happiness* (Grand Central Publishing, 2010), 236.

duration, but it's often the happiness we fixate upon: winning the lottery, getting engaged, getting the big promotion. After the excitement wanes, we are back at the baseline level we were before.

Passion, Hsieh says, is the type of happiness that occurs when we are at peak performance and engagement. We are at the top of our game, time seems to slow down, and we are in the moment. Athletes refer to being in "the zone," and writers and artists call it "flow." It's the second longest-lasting type of happiness.

Higher purpose is when we are connected to something beyond ourselves, when we are invested in something bigger than us. This is the happiness that lasts the longest.

One of the greatest gifts Sandi carries from her friendship with Tony Hsieh is that unwavering connection to being a part of something bigger than ourselves and focusing on the present moment, rooted in the gift of a higher purpose, trusting in the rhythm of whom you get to learn alongside as we work together to make the world a better place than we found it.

When we think about this framework, it correlates with another idea: where we land on the spectrum of *doing* and *being*. When we are in a constant state of doing, we are seeking some sort of stimuli to spike our dopamine levels. There's nothing wrong with that! Especially when we are also courting a state of being, a space in which we are not striving or seeking but rather appreciating the moment. We need both to exist and persist in the world, but sometimes the *doing* overtakes the *being*. Sometimes we get caught up in the tasks and the to-do lists and lose sight of the opportunities to just *be*—with our thoughts, in nature, or in the presence of others, without an agenda.

EVOLUTION OF NEEDS

Maslow's hierarchy of needs tells us that we need to have our basic needs (food, shelter, etc.) met before we can achieve more complex needs like success, self-actualization, and creativity. The chakra system reflects this as well. We must address our safety and security, which is reflected in the root chakra, before we can travel up the ladder to connect to our power, feel love and joy and ultimate bliss.

When we are safe and secure, we can operate from a place of groundedness. We are connected at our very core. When we are safe and secure in ourselves, we can begin to operate from a place of personal power. We tap into our personal superpowers, as we discussed in Chapter 7. When we are authentically living from our personal power, we can then begin to find connection and belonging based upon the most honest version of ourselves. This is the on-ramp to the joy highway!

To be clear, stepping into a space of joy and bliss isn't an achievement to be mastered. It isn't as though once you reach joy and bliss, cool, you're done; you've crossed the finish line. Life doesn't work that way. We are dynamic, constantly evolving beings. We are always learning new things about ourselves, and in so doing, have to revisit all the pitstops. You might be living in a pretty blissful state, and then you have a new baby. While this is something you've dreamt of and planned for, it is still a drastic change in your life, and may very well invite (or insist) that you revisit your old stories and beliefs or readdress your personal superpower. That doesn't mean you are backsliding, just that you are learning more and growing deeper. The goal isn't to reach an outcome, it is simply to recognize the importance of movement over stuckness.

STEPHANIE: TRAVELING WITH MY BLISS

After our sister trip to Austin, Stacie and Sandi had been talking about taking me to Bali with them for a global leadership and business growth training program. I have never been out of the country, so going to Bali was a huge thing for me. It was a major turning point not only in having the experience of traveling abroad for the first time but going into that whole new experience. Honestly, I was terrified, and I felt a pull backward in feeling overwhelmed and anxious all of the time. I was afraid to go because I let my "Am I worthy of this experience?" and my "What ifs?" take hold of me. I was irritated with myself for feeling this way, so I made a conscious choice. Two days before I got on the plane to go to Boston for the first leg of our trip to Bali, I decided my motto for this whole trip would be, "Fuck it." Because realistically, all I could do was just let go. I couldn't control any of the outcomes. I had to just ride whatever wave smacked me in the moment. That was the hardest part for me: getting out of my own way and allowing the waves to crash over me and then deal with them, move on, and come out of it stronger and better.

In Bali, as we visited Dream Beach, I was mesmerized by the continuous waves arriving on shore, which eventually buried my legs a foot deep in the sand. This was the universe saying, "Just take it, take the love, take the happiness. Just live in the moment." Take each moment and realize that, even if it's not on some beautiful dream beach, you still have these moments. These beautiful, fantastic, blissful, the "universe slaps you upside the head" moments that don't have to be traumatic or dramatic, like a car accident, but can be wonderful and amazing and beautiful. I found my bliss in that moment of surrender.

During the trip, I still had moments of questioning, and my motto alone was not enough to get me to a place of acceptance. At the Glass Bridge, I stood on the side, not wanting to cross the see-through walkway, and watched everybody scoot across in their little protective slippers. Watching everybody else enjoying the experience except for me, I had to ask myself, *What am I doing? Why am I here? I'm not here to stand on the sidelines and watch.* I realized this incident reflected my attitude toward all the aspects of my life. *I'm not here to stand on the sidelines and watch,* I repeated to myself. *I'm here to be in every moment, to love every moment, good or bad. I'm here to love myself. I'm here to love my children. I'm here to love my husband. I'm here to love my sisters. I'm here to be the best version of myself that I can be for myself and for every-one else I meet.* So I said, "Fuck it," and I made myself scoot across that glass bridge. I had to assert that motto in that moment and get out of my own way and comfort zone because life is not always comfortable. I felt a sense of progress, practicing every day to live intentionally.

Being in a car in Bali was not a fun time. Since the car accident, my anxiety often peaks as a passenger during times of significant traffic. Seeing motorbikes and cars navigating the roadways without clearly established lanes or stop signs felt chaotic. At one point, I had to have our taxi driver pull over and let me out of the car. I couldn't breathe, my limbs started tingling, and I could barely ask to get out of the car—I was in a full-blown panic attack. I was at a point where I could recognize the warning signs, and I have multiple coping tools to help me handle my car accident PTSD. But nothing was working. I sat on the side of the road on this little half wall and worked through it. My sisters were both there to love and support me, but ultimately, I had to do the work. I had to make the choice to focus on what was going well. In Bali, I saw that the world can go at a much slower pace, and I noticed that I have the control to slow my pace. This trip presented me with multiple opportunities to practice.

The Bali trip reminded me that we all have our individual struggles, ups and downs, ins and outs. Yet we are all on this crazy journey of life together. The trip also gave me the opportunity to sit and reflect, and I realized the importance of doing just that—stopping and breathing, and noticing the world around me and the people around me, the experiences that are happening right in front of me that I've always just pushed through because life is a constant push. Or is it? So that constant push for more is relative, fading in importance. When you're constantly striving for more and you're constantly only looking at the far-off picture or the light at the end of the tunnel, maybe you miss the beautiful graffiti that's all over the walls in that tunnel right in front of you—you miss your bliss.

Finding my bliss in Bali didn't make everyday life easy. Integrating back into my normal after the trip presented additional challenges. As I tried to explain the revelations from my trip to my family, they looked at me like I had three heads, like I was speaking a different language. I kept trying to tell them how I felt and how the culture in Bali had revealed wonderful insights. I wanted to integrate things that I had learned while in Bali into our home: being content and not always rushing everywhere, learning to just stop and breathe and not take everything for granted. They had no understanding of what I was talking about. So for me, everything started to become overwhelming. Everything felt hard. And then I remembered. I had to make myself stop, and I had to realize that it actually wasn't hard. It was just the fact that I had changed. And so I had to integrate my new attitudes, my new life, into my daily interactions with those I loved, creating a space "in the middle" that made everybody more comfortable so that I no longer appeared to have three heads and speak a different language. Little by little, my husband and kids began to understand and accept the new me, more often enveloped in a layer of calm, instead of the old me they had always known before, rushing around, enveloped in a whirlwind of frantic actions and negative attitudes.

I'm getting them to get out of their own heads and leave behind all of the negative occurrences. We know that life is hard. We're a double-divorced, blended family. We have four kids coming and going at all times. We have seven animals that always need something. There are many things that could cause us to be angry and frustrated. And yet, I repeat the mantra: *You can't control the outcome. You can't control anything but yourself.*

You can only control your actions and reactions, and that's it. So live with integrity and be okay with how you react and with what you're saying and what you're doing, and that's all you can do in life. That's it. You know that there are lots of shitty things in the world. But there are so many beautiful things too. And you must consciously choose, every day, to focus on those beautiful things. I'm practicing unpacking my bliss.

THE JOY DEFICIENCY

Have you ever found yourself in a situation in which you think, "I should be feeling joyful right now," and yet, you are feeling anything but joy? Or worse, you aren't feeling anything at all?

Many times, we suffer from a joy deficiency. This is sort of like a vitamin deficiency: you haven't gotten enough B12 in your system, so you have to take a supplement to get back to baseline healthy levels. Similarly, when you've experienced a great deal of grief or trauma in your life, you may be experiencing a joy deficiency. That's nothing to beat yourself up over; it's simply where you are at this moment in time.

What's the antidote to joy deficiency? Well, the first step, as we've discussed throughout this book, is radical acceptance of where you are in this moment. When you can lovingly be with yourself regardless of the circumstances, without guilt or shame for not feeling the way you "should" feel, you've taken a leap down the road to unpacking your bliss.

The second step is to increase your joy intake. Think about the times you remember feeling joyful or happy. What were you doing? Who were you with? How can you create an atmosphere of joy around yourself so that you can begin to infuse your system with the feeling of bliss again? Don't worry: much like riding a bike or remembering how to kiss, your body will remember what it feels like to experience joy when you give it a chance to practice.

The third step is to begin to recognize those small moments. Take note of them as they are happening. Take a pause to notice the details around you. Especially notice how happiness feels in your body. Just noticing can help you absorb the joy into your body and remember your inner self.

SANDI: THE STORY OF ENOUGH

In 2019, our business coach/colleague/soul sister Lisa Chastain asked me a question that was so monumental it has woven its way through our story ever since. During a coaching session, Lisa asked, "What is enough?" To be honest, I wasn't sure.

A couple years later, we found ourselves at a women's retreat in Zion National Park. Stacie was especially thrilled to be in this magnificent landscape that she had a deep connection to. She held the visual of slot canyons in her mind as a safe, connected natural place, although she had never physically been there. In her mind's eye, she would visualize reaching out and touching the stone walls, letting their solidity ground her. She was determined to hike in the slot canyons on this trip.

While we participated in some of the retreat activities, we also gave ourselves permission to follow our own bliss. Following that bliss took an interesting turn. Stacie had a flash of inspiration.

"What if we get someone to drive us out to the slot canyons, and we hike into them, and we put on our dresses and have an impromptu photoshoot?" she said, breathless with the anticipation of it. Typically, I was the one to spark and dream up the brilliant ideas, but I knew a great idea when I heard one. So we set out to make it happen.

Our guide met us on a very cold morning to drive us out to the slot canyons. All three of us, Stacie, myself, and our photographer friend, Casey, were bundled in coats, beanies, and scarves that we dug out of the trunk of my car. We then threw our backpacks into the back of this ATV, wrapped ourselves in blankets, buckled up, and set out full speed to our destination. Our driver was the chillest of dudes but drove like a maniac. We held on for dear life, and we laughed like crazy. We reached the slot canyons, hiked in, and pulled on dresses. We whirled, danced, climbed, and threw our hands into the air joyously. It was one of the most playfully joyful experiences either of us can remember.

As we careened along the edges of the cliffs along this adventure, flushed from the joy of being together, embodying the most beautiful versions of ourselves shoulder to shoulder, heart to heart, in the breathtaking beauty of the landscape, I gripped Stacie's hand.

"This is it. This is enough." And we have the photos to prove it.

We recognize that it took a lot to set the stage for that blissful moment, and we can use visualization to return to that moment at any given time. When days feel heavy, we can use this and other joyful moments to guide us back to bliss—a gentle nudge toward mindfulness.

THE REAL YOU IS BLISS

In his book, *The Ultimate Happiness Prescription*, Deepak Chopra writes:

> *Being present and experiencing presence are the same, and neither one requires effort. You cannot work to be present. You just are. If you practice mindfulness, this quality of joyful presence will begin to be with you all the time. If you find yourself getting distracted, just noticing that you are distracted will bring you back to the present. The kind of mindfulness I am talking about has nothing to do with emptiness, or checking out. It doesn't require concentration or intensity. It is the most relaxed and natural state because nothing is more relaxed than yourself. You can slip into it simply by noticing each distracting activity and letting it go. "Easy come, easy go" actually has a deep spiritual meaning. What comes and goes isn't the real you. The real you is the bliss that exists beyond time.* [18]

Bliss is our natural state of being. We are born able to experience an abundance of bliss. It is the programs that are handed down to us—in our evolutionary mindsets, our ancestral trauma, the programming from society or our family systems—that separate us from that state.

Throughout these pages, you have traveled a path that revealed

---

18   Deepak Chopra, *The Ultimate Happiness Prescription: 7 Keys to Joy and Enlightenment* (Random House, 2010).

how to unwind old beliefs and patterns, excavate old narratives, and delve into your values in order to ground your superpower. Now you can put this to use by giving yourself permission to be in the state of blissfulness at any given moment. What does bliss look like for *you*? Give yourself permission to create your own definition and to change it if you wish.

KEY NUGGETS:

- ∽ Authentic bliss doesn't always happen in the big experiences but in the micro moments, and that's totally normal.
- ∽ There are multiple levels of happiness.
- ∽ It's important to recognize our basic needs as we travel on the path to bliss.
- ∽ When we have experienced a period of struggle, we can find ourselves in a joy deficiency. The antidote: more fun, play, joy, and happiness!

You are not just meant to be in a state of bliss; *you are bliss. You simply get to rediscover the bliss within.* And practice connecting to the blissful moments nestled along the way. Pack those moments back in the suitcase—they are light and will travel well. When needed, simply *Unpack Your Bliss.*

Big Hugs!

REFERENCES

Brown, Brené. *Rising Strong: How the Ability to Reset Transforms the Way We Live, Love, Parent, and Lead.* New York: Random House, 2017.

Brown, Brené. *The Gifts of Imperfection: 10th Anniversary Edition.* New York: Simon & Schuster, 2022.

Center for Courage & Renewal, accessed November 16, 2022, https://couragerenewal.org.

Chopra, Deepak. *The Ultimate Happiness Prescription: 7 Keys to Joy and Enlightenment.* New York: Random House, 2010.

Dr. Darcy Lord, accessed April 24, 2022, *https://drdarcylord.com.*

Dispenza, Joe. *Breaking the Habit of Being Yourself.* Carlsbad, CA: Hay House, 2012.

Hanson, Rick, PhD. *Hardwiring Happiness: The New Brain Science of Contentment, Calm, and Confidence.* New York: Harmony Books, 2016.

Hsieh, Tony. *Delivering Happiness: A Path to Profits, Passion, and Purpose.* New York: Grand Central Publishing, 2013.

LaPorte, Danielle. *The Desire Map: A Guide to Creating Goals with Soul.* Louisville, CO: Sounds True, 2014.

Levine, Amir and Rachel Heller. *Attached. The New Science of Adult Attachment and How it Can Help You Find—And Keep—Love.* New York: TarcherPerigree, 2011.

Neff, Kristin. *Self-Compassion: The Proven Power of Being Kind to Yourself*. New York: HarperCollins, 2011.

Palmer, Parker J. *A Hidden Wholeness: The Journey Toward an Undivided Life*. Hoboken, NJ: Wiley, 2022.

Talent Dynamics Profile Test. Accessed June 15, 2022. https://human-izedu.com/talent-dynamics.

Walker, Pete. "Codependency, Trauma and the Fawn Response." *The East Bay Therapist*, Jan/Feb 2003. *https://pete-walker.com/codependencyFawnResponse.htm.*

ABOUT THE AUTHORS

Dr. Stacie Herrera

As the founder and CEO of Herrera Psychology and the Chief Impact Officer of HumanizEDU, Dr. Herrera is a licensed school psychologist dedicated to addressing the youth mental health crisis through systemic, innovative approaches. She engages diverse audiences in conversations about youth mental health, embracing neurodiversity, and uncovering unique purposes while emphasizing individual strengths. Dr. Herrera is deeply committed to fostering collaborative, child-centered environments where every stakeholder can thrive!

Sandi Herrera

As co-founder and CEO of HumanizEDU, Sandi Herrera is leading the movement to put humans back at the center of education. Through her work in the US and abroad, she strives to help schools become happy, empowering, and engaging places to work and learn! Sandi discovered her passion for developing strong workplace and school cultures while working as COO for Delivering Happiness, a firm established by the late Zappos CEO, Tony Hsieh. She has spent her entire career working with diverse populations to amplify the value of all humans and believes that when we ignite the genius in all of us, we can open the door to opportunities bigger than we could have ever imagined!

LEARN MORE

Your journey with *Unpacking Bliss: The Suitcase Theory of Life* doesn't have to end here! Meet Bliss, your personal guide to exploring the ideas and insights from the book. Scan the QR code to chat with Bliss, who will help you dive deeper, reflect on thought-provoking questions, and find practical ways to unpack your own "suitcase" for a more fulfilling life.

Bliss is here to make the journey even more rewarding—your next step to happiness is just a scan away!

www.ingramcontent.com/pod-product-compliance
Lightning Source LLC
Chambersburg PA
CBHW041929090426
42744CB00016B/1992